YALE LECTURES ON THE
RESPONSIBILITIES OF CITIZENSHIP

CONDITIONS OF PROGRESS IN
DEMOCRATIC GOVERNMENT

YALE LECTURES ON THE
RESPONSIBILITIES OF CITIZENSHIP
(UNIFORM WITH THIS VOLUME)

THE HINDRANCES TO GOOD CITIZENSHIP

BY THE RIGHT HON. JAMES BRYCE
BRITISH AMBASSADOR TO THE UNITED STATES

A SCHOLARLY AND SUGGESTIVE VOLUME ON THE
IMPEDIMENTS TO GOOD CITIZENSHIP

"The book should have a place by the side of 'The American Commonwealth' — no higher place were possible."
— *Worcester Evening Gazette.*

(Second printing.)   138 pages, index, 12mo. $1.15 net.
Postage 10 cents.

CONDITIONS OF PROGRESS IN DEMOCRATIC GOVERNMENT

BY

CHARLES EVANS HUGHES

NEW HAVEN: YALE UNIVERSITY PRESS
LONDON: HENRY FROWDE
OXFORD UNIVERSITY PRESS
MCMX

Copyright, 1910
BY
YALE UNIVERSITY PRESS

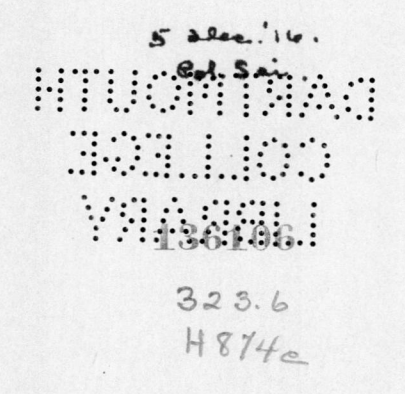

PRINTED IN THE UNITED STATES

CONDITIONS OF PROGRESS IN
DEMOCRATIC GOVERNMENT

LECTURE I

INTRODUCTION

Mr. President and Gentlemen of Yale University:

To you who are enjoying academic advantages and especially to those of you who are devoting yourselves to the study of history and political science, it must seem presumptuous for one who is under the pressure of the exacting duties of executive office to attempt to meet the requirements of a university lectureship. The invitation, with which I have been honoured, and my acceptance of it, can be justified only upon the ground that the chief intention of the founder of this course of lectures was not to invite scholastic disquisition, but rather to quicken in young men the sense of civic responsibility, and that this object might to some degree be attained if one in the midst of public work should seek to draw, though only in outline, a sketch of the field of endeavour, or privilege, of obligation.

I shall make, therefore, no effort to discuss theories of governmental systems, or to present an essay in constitutional history. In speaking of the responsibilities of citizenship, under the title of "Conditions of Progress in Democratic Government," I can give you only a point of view. I shall first speak on "The Attitude of the Individual," and later on "Administrative Efficiency," and "Political Parties."

THE ATTITUDE OF THE INDIVIDUAL

THE responsibilities of citizenship must not be regarded as limited to voting, to the use of electoral machinery, or to participation in political campaigns. These are simply methods to secure the expression of public opinion which is the final authority. Opportunity and the responsibility which it measures, with respect to citizenship, are to be determined not merely by particular political rights, but by one's relation to the ultimate power which upholds or changes constitutions, makes laws, fixes the quality of administration and assures or prevents progress.

Many are disturbed by the thought of the multitude of the unlettered and the regrettable number of besotted or debased who enjoy the equal privilege of the suffrage; and their own privilege and obligation are thus cast into disesteem. But this reflection should rather quicken the sense of responsibility and heighten the appreciation of opportunity. It is not merely that if one is dismayed by the number of others who count, he should be sure to count. This is a sobering thought, but there is much more. Equality of civil right secures necessary freedom of expression; but back of the votes are the influences which determine the votes, — the varied forces which produce conviction and create public sentiment. It is the extent to which one contributes, or may contribute, to these influences that measures political power.

The responsibilities of citizenship, then, embrace all those acts or possible acts, all those habits or attitudes, which express the totality of one's possible contributions to the formation of public opinion and to the maintenance of proper standards of civic conduct. Power and responsibility are to be judged not by the single vote, but by the indefinable influence radiating from personality, varying with moral perception, knowledge, acumen, experience, and environment, and capable of being lessened or increased, as one shrinks his individuality or expands his life and throws his full weight as a growing man of noble purpose into the civic scale.

When one is about to loose the ties of delightful association in college and to face a world of competitive efforts, he naturally asks himself, "What is to be my lot in life?" "Where shall I find a chance to prove what I can do?" "How shall I win for myself a place of security protected by my energy or ingenuity or thrift from the possible

IN DEMOCRATIC GOVERNMENT 5

assaults of misfortune?" "How can I achieve a competence or a fortune, or distinction?" For many, perhaps most, young men, the pressure of necessity is so strong, or ambition is so keen or the vision of opportunity is so alluring that these questions seem to transcend all others and too frequently suggest the dominant motive.

But there is another question, too rarely defined in conscious self-discipline, yet urged by a myriad of voices whose appeal dimly heard in the medley and confusion of the market-place sounds the deep tone of democracy, — "What shall be my attitude toward the community?" "How shall I relate myself to that struggling, achieving mass of humanity, — the people of this great country?" "What part shall I play, not as a unit fighting other units for individual advantage, but as a citizen of a Republic?"

Probably every one of you has been impressed with the forces of progress. I do not refer merely to those represented in production and exchange, significant as are these activities of an energetic and talented people. The large success and expansion of industry, the increase of wants and the ability to supply them, the extraordinary development in facilities of communication, are a sufficient answer to any who would speak of decadence in energy or will. But even more significant are the multiplying indications of earnest desire for the betterment of community life. I refer to the fine endeavours that are being made to extend and perfect the means of education; to improve conditions of labour; to secure better housing and sanitation; to stay the ravages of communicable disease; to provide proper care for the afflicted and defective in body and mind; to increase reformatory agencies and to improve penal methods to the end that society may protect itself without the travesty of making its prisons schools of crime; to secure higher standards of public service and a higher sense of loyalty to the common weal.

Slight consideration of the course of these endeavours emphasizes the lesson that progress is not a blessing conferred from without. It merely expresses the gains of individual efforts in counteracting the sinister and corrupting influences which, if successful, would make democratic institutions impossible. Gratifying as is the vast extent and variety of our accomplishment, one cannot be insensible to the dangers to which we are exposed. No greater mistake can be made than to think that our institutions are fixed or may not be changed

IN DEMOCRATIC GOVERNMENT

for the worse. We are a young nation and nothing can be taken for granted. If our institutions are maintained in their integrity, and if change shall mean improvement, it will be because the intelligent and the worthy constantly generate the motive power which, distributed over a thousand lines of communication, develops that appreciation of the standards of decency and justice which we have delighted to call the common sense of the American people.

Increasing prosperity tends to breed indifference and to corrupt moral soundness. Glaring inequalities in condition create discontent and strain the democratic relation. The vicious are the willing, and the ignorant are the unconscious instruments of political artifice. Selfishness and demagoguery take advantage of liberty. The selfish hand constantly seeks to control government, and every increase of governmental power, even to meet just needs, furnishes opportunity for abuse and stimulates the effort to bend it to improper uses. Free speech voices the appeals of hate and envy as well as those of justice and charity. A free press is made the instrument of cunning, greed, and ambition, as well as the agency of enlightened and independent opinion. How shall we preserve the supremacy of virtue and the soundness of the common judgment? How shall we buttress Democracy? The peril of this Nation is not in any foreign foe! We, the people, are its power, its peril, and its hope!

The causes of indifference to the obligations of citizenship may be traced in part to the optimistic feeling that nothing can go seriously wrong with us. This may indeed spring from belief in the intelligence and moral worth of the people, but that belief has ground only as there are predominant evidences of a growing sense of the duties imposed by democratic government, of an appreciation of responsibility enlarging apace with the seductions that are incident to material advancement. There is also the difficulty of realizing that government is not something apart from us, or above us, that it is we ourselves organized in a grand co-operative effort to protect mutual rights and to secure common opportunity and improvement. More potent still is the feeling of helplessness in the presence of organized agencies which, with their effective combinations based upon mutual interest, seem to make of slight consequence the efforts of citizens who are not members of inner circles of power. But no organized agency and no combination, however strong, can outrage the rights of any community, if the community sees fit to assert them. The character of the agencies of the community, its instruments of expression, the forms of its organized effort are simply what it may desire or tolerate. Whatever evil may exist in society or politics, simply points the question to the individual citizen, "What are you doing about it?"

Before we deal with particular problems and relations, I desire to consider the fundamental question of attitude and the principles of action which must be regarded as essential to the faithful discharge of the civic duties.

It is of first importance that there should be sympathy with democratic ideals. I do not refer to the conventional attitude commonly assumed in American utterances and always taken on patriotic occasions. I mean the sincere love of Democracy. As Montesquieu says: "A love of the republic in a democracy is a love of the democracy; as the latter is that of equality."

It would be difficult to find an association in which wealth, or family, or station are of less consequence, and in which a young man is appraised more nearly at his actual worth, than in an American college. Despite the increase of luxury in college living, the number of rich men's sons who frequent these institutions, and the amount of money lavishly and foolishly expended, our colleges are still wholesomely democratic. A young man who is decent, candid, and honourable in his dealings, will not suffer because he is poor, or his parents are obscure, and the fact that he may earn his living in humble employment in order to pay for his education will not cost him the esteem of his fellows. He will be rated, as the rich man's son will be rated, at the worth of his character, judged by the standards of youth which maintain truth and fair dealing and will not tolerate cant or sham. This is so largely true that it may be treated as the rule, and regrettable departures from it as the exception.

But a larger sympathy and appreciation are needed. The young man who goes out into life favourably disposed toward those who have had much the same environment and opportunity may still be lacking in the broader sympathy which should embrace all his fellow-countrymen. He may be tolerant and democratic with respect to those who, despite differences in birth and fortune, he may regard as kindred spirits, and yet in his relation to men at large, to the great majority of his fellow beings, be little better than a snob. Or despite the camaraderie of college intercourse he may have developed a cynical disposition or an intellectual aloofness which, while not marked enough to interfere with success in many vocations, or to disturb his conventional relations, largely disqualifies him from aiding his community as a public-spirited citizen. The primary object of education is to emancipate; to free from superstition, from the tyranny of worn-out notions, from the prejudices, large and small, which enslave the judgment. His study of history and of the institutions of his country has been to little purpose if the college man has not caught the vision of Democracy and has not been joined by the troth of heart and conscience to the great human brotherhood which is working out its destiny in this land of opportunity.

The true citizen will endeavour to understand the different racial viewpoints of the various elements which enter into our population. He will seek to divest himself of antipathy or prejudice toward any of those who have come to us from foreign lands, and he will try, by happy illustration in his own conduct, to hasten appreciation of the American ideal. For him "American" will ever be a word of the spirit and not of the flesh. Difference in custom or religion will not be permitted to obscure the common human worth, nor will bigotry of creed or relation prevent a just appraisement. The pitiful revelations of ignorance and squalor, of waste and folly, will not sap his faith. He will patiently seek truly to know himself and others, and with fraternal insight to enter into the world's work, to share the joys of accomplishment, and to help in the bearing of the burdens of misery. He will be free from the prejudice of occupation or of residence. He will not look askance either at city or at country. For him any honest work will be honourable, and those who are toiling with their hands will not be merely economic factors of work, but human beings of like passions and possessed of the "certain unalienable rights." Neither birth nor station, neither circumstance nor vocation, will win or prevent the esteem to which fidelity, honesty, and sincerity are alone entitled. He will look neither up nor down, but with even eye will seek to read the hearts of men.

This sense of sympathetic relation should increase respect both for individual interests and for community interests and should give a better understanding of what is involved in each. They are not in opposition; properly speaking they cannot be divorced. By individual interests I mean those interests which concern the normal development of the individual life, which relate to freedom in choice of work and individual pursuits, to the conservation of opportunities for the play of individual talent and initiative, to the enjoyment of property honestly acquired. The liberty of the individual in communities must of course be restrained by the mutual requirements imposed upon each by the equal rights of others, and by the demands of the common welfare. It may be difficult to define the precise limitations of such restrictions, but the guiding principle must be that the common interest cannot be preserved if individual incentive is paralyzed, and that to preserve individual incentive there must be scope for individual effort freely expended along lines freely chosen and crowned by advantages individually acquired and held. There is no alchemy which can transmute the poverty of individual hope into communal riches. Restrictions, to be justified, must be such as are essential to the maintenance of wholesome life and to prevent the liberty of some from accomplishing the enthraldom of all.

It is unfortunate that the claim of individual

rights has so frequently been asserted in the effort to protect unlawful gains and systematic pillaging of the community through abuse of public privileges. The wolf appears in sheep's clothing. The influence of just conservatism has often been lost, because so many wrongs parade in its livery. If no one were endeavouring to defend extortion and inadequate public service by the pretence of individual rights, if it were not sought to add to normal opportunities, abnormal and improper advantages obtained through special privilege, there would be far less disposition to press restrictions in the interest of the general community. But abuses should not blind us to good uses. And in prescribing the area of individual opportunity we must remember ever to prize as the essential condition of progress and human happiness the differentiation of effort based upon aptitude and the incentive to endeavour supplied by the enjoyment of the recompense won under honourable conditions.

Almost every man is solicitous for individual rights when he is thinking of his own. The true concern is for the interests of the individual as such, for that of another as well as for my own; that in the individual life of each member of society there should be zest and aspiration, and to all opportunity. Now, to maintain conditions which assure a fair field to all and protect each one from exploitation in the interest of those who may be entrusted with the operations of government, the people must have a keen sense of their collective interests. No one can properly discharge his duties as a citizen who simply has a good-natured feeling toward all, and merely wishes in a general way that every man shall prosper. This desire must be sharpened by a consideration of particular evils, and one must understand the necessity of co-operative vigilance. He must learn to make his personal decisions, as well as to define his public attitude, in the light of the interests of the community and not simply with respect to the opportunities for his individual gain. No allurement of high salary or of social advantage, no promise of assistance to obtain public office, should he permit to obscure his duty of absolute loyalty to the public interest. Trying to cheat the public is a game that is constantly being played, and if there is anything that is more dishonourable that can be thought of in one who has had the advantages of the higher institutions of learning, I do not know what it is. Sometimes it takes gross forms and falls clearly within the provisions of the penal law. But the citizen should have a higher notion of public duty than simply to keep out of jail. It is the less obvious and more subtle forms of treachery to the common interest against which the community must be constantly on its guard and from which the high-minded citizen will seek to keep his own life free. It is well to advise young men to vote and to take an active part in political affairs, but it is just as important, indeed more important, that they should understand that their first duty is so to conduct themselves in pursuing the aims of their individual careers that they will never prove false to their allegiance to the community. An intense consciousness of public relation should restrain the lawyer when he is tempted to go beyond his professional duty of presenting clearly and cogently the facts and arguments in favour of his client and to seek by trick or device to delay or defeat justice. It should make it impossible for managers of corporations to defend what they may believe to be their interests, either by paying blackmail or by endeavouring improperly to solicit the representatives of the people. It should stay the hand which would write surreptitious clauses in legislative bills or seek to secure privilege at public expense by indirection. It should give rise

IN DEMOCRATIC GOVERNMENT 17

to the same sense of honour in dealings which may affect the public as animates the true gentleman in his private relations. With respect to every governmental relation there is need to stimulate the sentiment which appreciates the common interest, demands its recognition, and prompts one to yield to it ungrudgingly, though it come in conflict with individual ambition.

There will be sincere debate as to where the line of demarcation between proper private enterprise and public duty should be drawn. But the field is so large in which the supremacy of public interest is theoretically admitted, that it is of the utmost practical importance to cultivate the sense of responsibility as to these recognized collective rights, and to make it no less keen than that which is felt with regard to the rights of the individual.

The increase of population has revealed the necessity for many protective measures. In the early days the hardy pioneer penetrated the forests and was compelled to make a clearing in order that he might establish a settlement. The sound of the axe was the first note of approaching civilization. The woods were a barrier to be destroyed. But when settlements multiplied and population increased and the forests had largely disappeared, we awoke to a realization that in the wooded hills was nature's choicest gift, with the preservation of which is linked our future prosperity. The interests of all demand that we should acquire and cherish a collective right, and that individual opportunity so far as it may threaten the maintenance of our forests should be taken away. Until recently little thought has been paid to our water-courses. They have been regarded as the natural conduits for human and industrial wastes; but as our growth threatens to make them mere sewers, the necessity for the assertion of collective rights, in order that our streams may remain wholesome, has become apparent. We are giving attention to the safeguarding of public health by segregating disease and limiting the opportunities of contagion. The great white plague takes toll of the energy and economic efficiency of this country with an appalling death-rate which may be largely reduced by insistence on suitable precautions. The public is entitled to protection from the adulteration of foods, from impurities in water, milk, meat, and other essential supplies. In our large communities no one can live unto himself. The condition of the tenement is a matter of consequence not simply to those who live in it, and sanitary safeguards are essential to the interest of all. We are learning to appreciate our interdependence with respect to industrial efficiency. If we are to progress as a nation we must take care of childhood. We must not only protect it against disease and secure child life from injurious or too early occupation, but we must also provide, in breathing space and playgrounds, for a wholesome youth fitted to enter into the activities of our expanding life. The maintenance of decent conditions of labour and of safeguards against loss of life and limb are in the interest of industrial progress and the achievement of a larger general prosperity. Schemes of public education are being modified by the introduction of trade schools and increased opportunity for vocational training. There has also arisen an irresistible demand that better means should be provided for the enforcement of public rights; that the creatures of the State receiving privileges from the public should be compelled to obey the laws of their being. Protest against inadequate service, the scandals that have arisen from the laying of excessive burdens upon the public, in order to pay dividends upon inflated issues of securities, have resulted in the conviction that there must be suitable machinery for scrutinizing and determining the propriety of issues of stocks and bonds, for the prompt examination of complaints as to the performance of public duty, for suitable investigation of complicated facts relating to rates, charges, and service, to the end that through competent means the public right should be enforced. These are important illustrations of the movement in the direction of better protection of the interests of the community.

The lover of democracy will have no desire to see the tyranny of despots replaced by the tyranny of a majority taking unto itself the conduct of individual life and the destruction of its hope. He knows that no community can be free if its members are deprived of liberty. But he also knows that he will utterly fail to find the sure basis for his liberty, under our social conditions, in his independent action, and that this foundation must be secured by intelligent co-operation. To save society from overreaching and impoverishing itself by arbitrary interference and at the same time to uphold the public right as supreme, to secure the benefits of collective effort while wisely safeguarding individual opportunity and initiative, is the patriotic and difficult task which should enlist the best thought and unselfish endeavour of every citizen who appreciates the advantages and the dangers of the Republic.

In all its efforts, democracy will make progress in the degree that the people cultivate the patience and steadiness of justice. The obligations of citizenship are not to be met by spasmodic outbursts or by feverish demonstrations of public interest. It is true that we make our most important choices of the representatives of the people amid the tumult of exaggerated and interested appeals. To a superficial observer the excitements of a political campaign would seem to imply the dethronement of reason. But it is to the credit of our people that they are so largely deliberative and have proved themselves so well able to sift the chaff from the wheat in political arguments, and are so skilful in following the thread of truth through the maze of prejudiced assertion and cunning perversion. If we were governed by gusts of passion and lost our heads in the turmoil of political strife, our freedom would be a travesty.

The desire to know the truth and to deal fairly with men and measures is of the essence of good citizenship. The most dangerous foes of democratic government are those who seek through special privilege to pervert it to selfish uses, and those who, by reckless, untruthful, and inflammatory utterances, corrupt the public sentiment. The more dangerous is the latter. For the motive power of any remedial effort must be found in public opinion, and to achieve good results it must be just. There are those who take a poor view of our prospects because of the recklessness of the sensational press. It is difficult for them to conceive that the community can steady itself against these constant and insidious assaults upon its judgment and sense of proportion. If indeed the people believed all they read and their mental attitude and emphasis were accurately reflected in headlines and type, it would seem cause for despair. But those who are pessimistic with regard to the influence of certain portions of the press fail to take account of the many forces that determine public sentiment. The habit of exaggeration furnishes to a large degree its own corrective, and its sensational exhibitions are taken seriously by few. The average man is very curious, and the fact that his curiosity will tempt him to buy and read does not necessarily indicate that what he has read has made much of an impression. Men are in constant communication with each other, in the shop, in the office, in going to and from their work, in the family, in their varied social relations, and in this intercourse information and opinions derived from many sources are freely interchanged. Their experience of life largely determines their point of view. What is read with regard to men and measures is generally accepted or rejected not upon mere assertion, but as it may or may not accord with the general opinions which experience has produced. This fact points the lesson that the most serious consequences of breaches of public trust and of corruption in high places are not to be found in the particular injuries inflicted, but in the undermining of the public confidence and in the creating of a disposition to give credit to charges of similar offending. But, as has been said, much of reckless and disproportionate statement, much of malicious insinuation, much of frenzied and demagogical appeal, fails of its mark.

While we may be grateful for this, and fully appreciate that with the spread of education this capacity of the people to resist such assaults will tend to increase, we cannot but be sensible of the evil influence that is actually exerted. To combat this and to maintain in the community standards of candour and justice should be the aim of every citizen.

If it be asked how an individual can accomplish aught in this direction, it may be answered that it lies with the individual to accomplish everything. The man who demands the facts, who is willing to stand or fall by the facts, who forms his convictions deliberately and adheres to them tenaciously, who courts patient inquiry and "plays fair," is a tower of strength in any group to which he may be related. We have no greater advantage than a free press and the freedom of public utterance. We would not lose its benefits because of its abuses. Demagoguery will always have a certain influence, and the remedy is to be found not in repression or impatient denunciation, but in the multiplication of men of intelligence who love justice and cannot be stampeded.

The citizen should contribute something more than sympathy with democracy, something more than respect for individual and community interests, something more than adherence to the standards of fair dealing. Sympathy and sentiment will fail of practical effect without independence of character. A man owes it to himself so to conduct his life that it be recognized that his assent cannot be expected until he has been convinced. He should exhibit that spirit of self-reliance, that sense of individual responsibility in forming and stating opinion, which proclaims that he is a man and not a marionette. This of course is a matter of degree varying with personality and depends for its beneficial effect upon intelligence and tact. None the less, the emphasis is needed. There are so many who with respect to public affairs lead a life largely of self-negation! They are constantly registering far below their capacity and never show anything like the accomplishment for which they were constructed and equipped. We have too many high-power vessels whose power is never used.

It is constantly urged that men must act in groups and through organizations to accomplish anything. This is obviously true and describes such a marked tendency that it is hardly necessary to point the lesson. The difficulty is not to get men to act in groups and through organization, but to have groups and organizations act properly and wisely by reason of the individual force and independent strength of their members. Groups and organizations constantly tend to represent the influence and power of one man or a few men, who are followed not because they are right, but because they lead, and who maintain themselves not so much by the propriety and worth of leadership as by their skill and acumen in availing themselves of the indifference of others and by use of solicitations, blandishments, and patronage. This is illustrated in all forms of association, and to the extent that it exists, the association loses its strength and capacity to accomplish the results for which it is intended. Groups and organizations within democracy depend upon the same conditions as those which underlie the larger society. If they come into the strong control of a few by reason of the indifference and subservience of the many, the form is retained without the substance and the benefits of co-operative action are lost.

It is of course a counsel of wisdom that men should be tactful and desirous of co-operating, and not in a constant state of rebellion against every effort at group action. But men who are eccentric and impossible are proof against counsel; and their peculiarities simply illustrate the exceptional and abnormal in society. The normal man naturally tends to work with others; to him the sentiment of loyalty makes a powerful appeal. And the counsel that is most needed is that men in the necessary action of groups should not lose their individual power for good by blind following. The man who would meet the responsibilities of citizenship must determine that he will endeavour justly, after availing himself of all the privileges which contact and study afford, to reach a conclusion which for him is a true conclusion, and that the action of his group shall if possible not be taken until, according to his opportunity and his range of influence, his point of view has been presented and considered. This does not imply sheer obstinacy or opinionated stubbornness. Progress consists of a series of approximations. But it does imply self-respect, conscientious effort to be sound in opinion, respect for similar efforts on the part of others, and accommodations in the sincere desire for co-operative achievement which shall be rational and shall be sensibly determined in the light of all facts and of all proposals. It also implies that there shall be no surrender that will compromise personal integrity or honour, or barter for gain or success one's fidelity to the oath of office or to the obligation of public trust.

A consideration of the obstacles which are found to be successfully interposed to this course is not flattering to those of our citizens who have had the greatest advantages. There is, in the first place, the base feeling of fear. Lawyers are afraid that they will lose clients; bankers, that they will lose deposits; ministers, that important pew-holders will withdraw their support; those who manage public service corporations, that they will suffer retaliation. Throughout the community is this benumbing dread of personal loss which keeps men quiet and servile.

The first lesson for a young man who faces the world with his career in his own hands is that he must be willing to do without. The question for him at the start and ever after must be not simply what he wants to get, but what he is willing to lose. "Whosoever shall lose his life shall preserve it," is the profoundest lesson of philosophy. No one can fight as a good soldier the battles of democracy who is constantly seeking cover.

But still more influential is the desire to avoid controversy and to let things go. The average American is good-hearted, genial, and indisposed not simply to provoke a quarrel, but even to enter into a discussion. By the constant play of his humour he seeks to avoid sharp contacts or expression of differences. But independence of conviction and the exercise of one's proper influence do not imply either ill-nature or constant collisions with opposing forces. The power of the man who is calm and temperate, just and deliberate, who seeks to know the truth and to act according to his honest convictions, is after all not best figured by the force of arms, but by the gracious influence of sunshine and of rain and the quiet play of the beneficent forces of nature. In suitably expressing his individuality, in presenting his point of view, he need not sacrifice his geniality or the pleasures of companionship which are always enhanced by mutual respect.

Then there are the fetters of accumulated obligations. The strongest appeal that can be made to an American is to his generous sense of obligation because of favours received. Men whom no wealth could bribe and no promise could seduce will fall in public life victims to a chivalrous regard for those who have helped them climb to public place. This is because of a strange inversion of values. The supposed private debt is counted more important than the public duty. But there are no obligations which friendship or kindly action can impose at the expense of public service. It is simply a perverted sentiment which suggests such a demand or the necessity of meeting it. It is a strange notion, which courses in ethics and the benefits of higher education so frequently find it difficult, if not impossible, to dislodge.

Whether you like it or not, the majority will rule. Accept loyally the democratic principle. The voice of the majority is that neither of God nor of devil, but of men. Do not be abashed to be found with the minority, but on the other hand do not affect superiority or make the absurd mistake of thinking you are right or entitled to special credit merely because you do not agree with the common judgment. Your experience of life cannot fail to impress you with the soundness of that judgment in the long run, and I believe you will come to put your trust, as I do, in the common sense of the people of this country, and in the verdicts they give after the discussions of press, of platform and of ordinary intercourse. The dangers of the overthrow of reason and of the reign of passion and prejudice become serious only as resentment is kindled by abuses for which those who have no sympathy with popular government and constantly decry what they call "mob rule" are largely responsible. But whether the common judgment shall exhibit that intelligence and self-restraint which have given to our system of government so large a degree of success, will depend upon your attitude and that of the young men of the country who will determine the measure of capacity for self-government and progress in the coming years.

Prize your birthright and let your attitude toward all public questions be characterized by such sincere democratic sympathy, such enthusiasm for the common weal, such genuine love of justice, and such force of character, that your life to the full extent of your talent and opportunity shall contribute to the reality, the security, and the beneficence of government by the people.

LECTURE II

ADMINISTRATIVE EFFICIENCY

WHEN we cease to regard government as an abstraction and endeavour to understand its actual working, we cannot fail to be impressed with the rapidly increasing extent of its activities. The trouble with most of our study of civic government in our schools is that the mere endeavour to memorize names of offices and departments and to be prompt with definitions of powers and official relations, is so great a task that the ordinary student largely fails to get the impression of a vital and responsible relation to his government. Knowing the leading facts and divisions of administration is of course essential to the larger understanding of the matter; but it is this larger understanding and sense of vital relation that is the important thing.

To make profitable the study of detail, there should first be the comprehensive view to quicken interest in every part. Just as the traveller will climb a height to command an entire sweep of

IN DEMOCRATIC GOVERNMENT 33

range and valley and to secure a vivid impression of the configuration of the whole to guide him in his more minute local observations, so the intelligent citizen should have a vision of governmental activity, its course and tendency, and thus find greater zest and profit in local surveys.

A vast amount of work is being carried on by representatives of the people having defined functions. To have this work well done is nine-tenths of our task as citizens. The actual conduct of government, as distinguished from its theoretical scheme, is the severest test of democracy. The surest ground of criticism has always been that a single individual "performs the duties which he undertakes much better than the government of the community;" and democratic government has been unfavourably compared with monarchy because it is said that the government of an individual "is more consistent, more persevering, more accurate than that of a multitude, and it is much better qualified judiciously to discriminate the characters of the men it employs." We might well afford to suffer some disadvantage as to this for the sake of certain conspicuous benefits, but our thought and energies should be devoted to the task of reducing the disadvantage to the minimum. The larger part of our political discussion centres in legislative proposal and pertains to the amendment of the law. But important as improvement of the law may be, it must not be forgotten that the matter of chief consequence at all times is the conduct of government under the laws that we have.

The recent increase in the activities of government is not only notable in itself, but by reason of the prospect that is afforded of still further increases. I have already given some illustrations of the protective measures which have been adopted by the community, and what I wish now to emphasize is the transcendent importance of efficiency in view of the extent of the governmental work that is required. We are undertaking new tasks, and even with respect to old categories governmental activities are assuming an unparalleled scope.

The conservation of natural resources involves the creation of great preserves, the conduct of scientific forestry on a large scale, and the control and development of water-powers. Public works of enormous proportions are undertaken by Nation, State, and City. At this moment the Nation is digging a canal through the Isthmus of Panama; the State of New York is expending without federal assistance a hundred million dollars in a canal project which rivals that of the Isthmus in extent and difficulty; and the city of New York is establishing a system of water-supply, based upon reservoirs in the Catskill mountains, at a cost of upwards of one hundred and sixty million dollars. Plans for extensive development in highway construction, in irrigation and reclamation, and in the improvement of water-ways are either in progress or are submitted for serious consideration. The protection of the public health in connection with sanitation, purification of streams, and supervision of food supplies requires not simply the passage of laws, but elaborate provision for engineering work, for inspection, and for the varied duties of state and local health officers.

The equipment of governmental departments or bureaus to aid in the enforcement of the laws has been a marked feature of recent legislation. The modest provision at first made is generally found to be inadequate, and in order that the bureau may accomplish the purpose of its creation the necessity of an enlarged force becomes apparent. The expansion of business closely related to the public interest and the general appreciation of the importance of supervision, increase the demands upon government and the multiplication of agents. The growth of supervisory departments such as those relating to banks and insurance companies, and the creation and the enlargement of the powers of departments and commissions dealing with public service corporations are especially noteworthy. Experience has shown that if public supervision and regulation are to be adequate they must be made adequate by suitable administrative machinery, and this implies a proper complement of public officers. The promotion of agriculture has led to the establishment of special departments, federal and state. Agricultural colleges have been provided; government stations prosecute research and conduct experimental farms; the effort is made to disseminate among farmers the results of a wide experience; and special bureaus of inspection and prosecution are maintained. Similarly labour departments have been established in order to make sure that the provisions of law for the protection of labour do not become a dead letter; and these have special bureaus for the collection of statistics, for the inspection of factory and mercantile establishment, and for mediation and arbitration.

Public charities, in the technical sense of the term, have always made heavy demands upon

IN DEMOCRATIC GOVERNMENT 37

government, but there has been a remarkable increase of these demands in the past few years. It is agreeable to note the rapidly growing number of men and women who are interested in philanthropy, and they are constantly studying means of improvement. The old custodial methods, under which the unfortunate were herded together with slight regard for anything beyond segregation, are in course of abandonment. Modern philanthropy demands suitable provision for treatment, for occupation, for recreation. Youthful offenders are now being placed on large tracts of agricultural land, and are being provided for in groups of cottages where reformatory measures may be more successful. These improvements imply more extensive plants and additional employees. New lines of effort have been entered upon, as for example in the State of New York, in the Craig Colony for Epileptics at Sonyea, in the hospital at Raybrook for those suffering from incipient tuberculosis, in the cancer laboratory at Buffalo. The charitable and reformatory work of government is being revolutionized by new ideas, or by old ideas aided through the discoveries of science and enforced by more intense love of humanity.

Relatively the increased burden of governmental

work is heaviest at the weakest point of our system; that is, in our municipalities, particularly in our large cities. Municipal administration has had to cope with the demands due to the rapid growth and congestion of population.

Now if the citizen will realize this, and, not content with merely knowing the names of offices and divisions, will try to understand the import of this vast governmental activity in a democracy, he must be convinced that efficiency is no longer to be thought of as simply a theoretical obligation, defaults in which entail only negligible losses, but that it is a practical matter of first consequence, and that with respect to the maintenance of its proper standards each individual in the community should feel his responsibility.

The execution of the laws is commonly associated with prosecutions for criminal offences, for the sanction of laws defining public duties is generally found in the penalties enforced in the criminal courts. But the execution of the laws involves much more than punishment of criminal guilt. It embraces the execution of a host of measures demanding executive competence, careful management, the intelligent use of power, the just settlement of a myriad of administrative problems and the infusion of the public service with the spirit of faithful work. The head of a department should not be, as too frequently has been the case, a merely titular functionary who holds the office for the sake of the salary and is content with the irreducible minimum of routine work. Rather should he be one who, fitted by aptitude and training for his work, understands it, devotes his best energies to it, is able to evoke pride and zeal in deputies and subordinates, who constantly seeks to avoid unnecessary outlays, to introduce talent into the service, to ascertain flaws in the governmental machinery, and by faithful stewardship to make a good showing to his employers, the people. Public enterprise requires managerial capacity of a high order.

If there were no other reason for insisting upon efficiency, it should be sufficient to point out that the cost of government is increasing at a tremendous rate. Inefficiency is simply waste of public money; taxation to supply waste is nothing but extortion. This not only causes loss with respect to particular outlays; it prevents progress. Economy is not a popular watchword with the people at large. Campaign talk about the extravagance of government has, in large communities, a very limited effect, because people generally fail to appreciate that they are paying the bills, and that the real taxpayer is not necessarily the land-owner or the one who makes return to the assessor. But when they are denied public improvements to which they think they are entitled, they know it. Waste which loads down a budget with unnecessary appropriations and stands in the way of needed public improvements, provokes discontent, none the less a serious menace because the true obstacle to progress is so little understood. And if we are to have contented communities and be free from disorder, we must stop extravagance and careless expenditure and have the public business properly transacted. Thrift in communities is just as essential to happiness as thrift in the home. A community well governed in the sense that reasonable amounts derived by taxation are faithfully and intelligently expended will almost inevitably be a community of order and peace.

Efficient administration is also necessary to reveal defects in government, and to point the proper direction of remedial efforts. We cannot tell what is needed until what we have has been well tried. We are frequently in a state of confusion as to results because the experiments in the public laboratory are so carelessly conducted. The best plans of progress will be shattered if administration is faulty. And it is hardly worth while to consider improvements unless at the same time we insist upon having public work attended to with absolute fidelity and with the highest degree of ability that we can command.

When we consider the obstacles to efficiency in administration we find that the fundamental difficulty is the lax view that is taken of public obligation. The people are willing to tolerate in public employment what they will not tolerate in their own enterprises. If a man is rated as a good fellow, if he cannot be proved guilty of stealing, if he is a good father and a kindly neighbour, then there are many who consider it a great injustice that he should be adjudged guilty of gross waste and inexcusable inefficiency in the public work committed to him. When upon these grounds he becomes the subject of criticism, his friends — excellent persons — will assure you that he has not grown rich at public expense, as though that were an answer. Very likely his pastor will most sincerely plead for him because his private life is believed to be without reproach. It seems to be so difficult for many to realize that no one is entitled to be paid from the public treasury simply for being sober and honest.

and that while honesty and sobriety are essential, the public officer is paid for work and the people are entitled to have it well and economically done. Fortunately the idea is gaining ground, and with higher standards we may hope to reach the point where we can assume that officers will not steal or use their positions for the sake of personal gain, and we can centre our attention upon the qualifications which ensure thoroughness and expertness.

Apart from the indulgence with which administration has been viewed, there are several hindrances to efficiency which demand special consideration on the part of the citizen if he is intelligently to exercise his influence.

One is the inadequacy of laws. I have already referred to the obvious fact that legislation is not a substitute for administration, and that it is a frequent mistake to suppose that law is needed instead of the enforcement of law. Still, imperfect legislation frequently prevents the securing of benefits to which the people are entitled and which they have endeavoured to secure. When proposals are made for amendment of the law the familiar objection is that we have too much law. Certainly the activity of our legislators has appalling results when we consider the number of statutes which each legislative session produces, and the extent of unnecessary legislation is deplorable. But the thoughtful citizen will not turn a deaf ear to suggestions for improvement because he is told that there is too much law. He will understand that the real trouble is that there is too much ill-considered legislation. He will also appreciate the fact that careless law-making makes corrective legislation necessary. In addition, the impossibility of foreseeing all the cases that may arise in varied experience, makes it necessary to amend the law to meet the unexpected situation. Instead of impatiently disposing of all suggestions upon the ground that there is "too much law," he will be anxious to consider where the difficulty resides in the particular case, how it should be met, and the merits of the proposal made. Then he will be able deliberately to judge whether legislation is needed, and if so he will approve it. There is just as much folly in conservative epigram as in radical watchwords. In every case we must endeavour to find where the truth lies and to decide wisely according to the facts. While insisting, therefore, upon proper administration of existing laws, we should constantly be keen to ascertain what embarrassments are occasioned by imperfect laws.

There has also been a tendency to cripple administrative officers by laws that are too minute. One of the chief causes for prolific legislation is the constant necessity for adjusting laws to the expanding need of municipalities that are living under special acts. Usually we meet the situation by altering a link in the chain, or by changing a clasp, which must be changed again in another year because of some other exigency. In the desire to maintain liberty and to protect themselves from the abuse of administrative discretion, legislatures bind communities and officers with unnecessary bonds. This is true also with respect to constitutional limitations upon legislative power. Instead of providing a general charter of powers and broad limitations securing the essentials of republican government, the tendency is noticeable to multiply detailed restrictions so that our constitutions expand significantly with each convention.

Now it is true that in the unchecked discretion of legislatures and administrative officers lie the opportunities of tyranny. But on the other hand there is no greater mistake than to withhold the power to do well in the fear of ill. There is no adequate power that cannot be abused. But we must endeavour to find a remedy against abuse short of making official and administrative power inadequate. Communities should not be hampered with respect to matters that exclusively concern them. Instead of filling charters with minute restrictions as to local administration, there should be left to local authorities suitable opportunity to administer local affairs. This stimulates the public spirit of the locality and quickens the sense of public duty which is the mainspring of good government.

It probably is the opinion of the average citizen that the greatest obstacle to administrative efficiency is official corruption. There is undoubtedly sufficient reason why the vigilance of the people should be heightened and not relaxed. The purchase of public officers, the sale of indulgences to law-breakers to enhance the fortunes of those who control appointments to office, systematic levies for official favours, — these are crimes of the first magnitude, with respect to which every citizen should be swift to turn informer and every effort should be made to punish the guilty. But I believe that the grosser forms of corruption are happily more rare. There is less direct bribery and stealing. Corrupting influences have become more insidious, and for this reason are perhaps more dangerous.

They are rarely susceptible of proof; they leave few traces and largely defy investigation. These are the influences which are shown in the play of favouritism, in the payment of private obligations through official discretion, in permitting information to be given in advance of official action to those who may profit by the knowledge, in making administrative offices centres of solicitations which imply official promises. Larceny and embezzlement have largely given place to conspiracies and shrewd agreements for mutual protection and enrichment. Akin to these evils is the blighting influence of efforts to support partisan workers at the public expense, to which I shall refer later in connection with the matter of party organization. This practice not only affords the means through which administrative action is perverted in order to hold and to pay for political support, but it also forms the avenue for the introduction of incompetents into the public service and leads to the multiplication of unnecessary places. Partisan incumbrances to a great extent account for administrative palsy.

There is also the disposition to regard public employment as a refuge for those who cannot otherwise support themselves. Now public service

IN DEMOCRATIC GOVERNMENT 47

is not an almshouse, although the management of almshouses is an important branch of administration. It is no recommendation to an applicant for a place on the public payroll that he can get no other employment. Appointing officers do not receive their power to disburse the public moneys in order that they may dispense them in charity outside of institutions duly provided. The needy and the unfortunate should be cared for otherwise. This of course should not be taken to mean that men do not sometimes become available for public service through personal hardships and the vicissitudes of fortune. But the appointment must rest upon the ground of fitness, and need of the money is not a sufficient reason for selection.

The mere statement of some of these causes of defects in administration has involved suggestions as to the remedies that may be applied. But there are certain means of improving conditions which I desire to emphasize.

Every effort should be made to dignify public office. Instead of carping at the employee of the State as one who feeds at the public crib, there should be a keener realization of the necessity and importance of the work that is to be done and of the credit that attaches to the proper doing of it.

It has been thought that public office might be dignified by increasing its emoluments. Certainly many public officers are underpaid and work of an extent and quality is expected of them which private enterprise would not think of attempting to command upon like terms. The scale of compensation in many cases frequently reflects the standards of earlier days when the cost of living was less and the opportunities of receiving greater rewards were not so many. The public can afford to pay its servants decently, and, in the main, must do so if it is to maintain proper standards of public work.

In the great majority of places in the public service, particularly in those concerned with routine or technical work, the employment should be permanent. There is little chance of promotion, and the ordinary opportunities afforded in private business are largely lacking. This is a reason why employees of this description should be paid according to a scale certainly not below that governing payments for private work of the same sort. The efficiency of a force in a great department cannot be secured if men are recruited for it who are not qualified for, and hence cannot obtain, similar work elsewhere, who rankle under injustice and to whom the head of the department must apply his spur in vain. Good treatment and reasonable compensation are essential to good results.

But when we come to the higher offices I am not one of those who think that mere increases of salary will prove an adequate solution of the problem. I also share the feeling that we should be cautious about increasing the chance of drawing men to the public service who seek it for the sake of the compensation. It is idle to suppose that emoluments can be given which can rival those obtainable by men of first rate ability in their lines of chosen effort. Attorneys-general cannot be paid what is received by leaders of the bar; heads of banking and insurance departments cannot expect the compensation paid to the presidents of banks and insurance companies; judges must be content to serve for annual pay less in amount than may be received in a single case by the lawyers arguing before them. Men of eminent ability must be found to conduct the delicate work of supervising our great public service companies for rewards which are slight in comparison with those of the managers and officers of such corporations.

The difficulty is not insurmountable. The public should pay fair compensation and should not demand unreasonable sacrifices from those who serve it, but to attract good men and to secure efficiency, the honour and independence of the office are of far greater account than the emoluments that attach to it. If it be understood that the administrative head has proper freedom, that he will not be controlled by political organizations, that he will not be required to parcel out places that he is free to fill in order to satisfy the henchmen of political leaders, that he can organize his department on the basis of efficiency and receive credit from a public that is anxious to do honour to a public officer of conspicuous merit, there will be much less difficulty in attracting men of distinguished ability, as well as of the highest character, to the service of the State. While we recognize the fact that very large rewards are won in business enterprise and in professional employment by the exceptional few, we also know that there are many of first-class ability who, for reasons not to their disparagement, do not receive them. There are also public-spirited men of independent means, who are anxious to serve the State if the service can be rendered under honourable conditions. I know the difficulty of finding men who are available, who possess the requisite ability without being embarrassed by such relations

IN DEMOCRATIC GOVERNMENT 51

as impair the public confidence in the single-mindedness of their work, and who at the same time are willing to assume heavy official burdens. And I believe that the most important contribution that can be made to administrative efficiency is to promote the independence of officers and to attach to the office the degree of honour, which is commensurate with the importance of the work to be performed. The placing of inferior men in public office not only causes immediate loss, but cheapens the office itself; and every efficient officer who meets the requirements of his place not only accomplishes much in his immediate service, but powerfully aids in elevating his office to its true rank in the public estimate.

In considering this question, the obligation of fairness in the criticism of public officials becomes manifest. Criticism is the safeguard of the public; no intelligent officer would dispense with it if he could. It is the life current of democracy. But everyone who wields the critical pen or indulges in critical utterances should keenly feel his responsibility. We have a government of laws and not of men, but a government after all is nothing but men. To create a disinclination for public life, to make men feel that its conditions with regard to self-respect and decent reputation are intolerable, to drive men of sensibility away from its opportunities in sheer disgust, and to leave public employment the more accessible to adventurers, to soldiers of fortune, and to political hangers-on, is to fetter progress and to put a premium upon inefficiency.

I do not defend the supersensitive. A public officer should not wear his heart upon his sleeve, and should not take too seriously the flings of his opponents. If he is right he can afford to ignore them, and if he is wrong, he has little reason to complain. But when we have in mind the attracting of men to the public service and the securing of the proper conduct of public business, we cannot fail to recognize the great importance of candour and fairness in public comment. Giving credit where credit is due, establishing public office in honourable estimation is to a large degree to assure fidelity and to minimize the temptations of the public officer to seek other rewards.

Some of you probably will go into journalism and you will justly rejoice in the opportunities it affords. You will recognize the great advantage of the impersonal character of most of its work, and I hope you will also realize the obligations of decency and honour, and that you will no more circulate an untruthful statement or a reckless statement with regard to a public officer than you would be guilty of treachery to the flag in time of war. A man who seeks profit in the sale of calumnies is the most despicable of human creatures. On the other hand, accurate accounts of public affairs with just praise or blame, or at least with a sincere desire to be just in praise or blame, the careful pointing out of what has been done and what should be done, the effort to understand the situation and to depict it truthfully, to give fidelity its due reward of public credit and faithlessness the severe censure it deserves, — this is work of a high order. Every citizen has it in his power to contribute to the maintenance of proper standards of criticism, and to swell the rebuke of those who abuse their privileges.

I have often been asked whether a young man should seek a public career and should make public office an object of ambition. Readiness to take office on the part of those who are qualified for it and are so circumstanced that they can take it, is one of the requisites of increased efficiency. There is no higher ambition than to be of public service; and to hold public office in order to be of service is an aim to be honourably cherished. The first consideration is that no one should take office, or pursue it, where his taking or pursuit will involve any obligations detrimental to the faithful execution of his duties. If one has the ambition to follow a public career he should distinctly perceive that it must not be allowed to dominate self-respect or to supplant the ideals of citizenship. Every young man should aim at independence and should prepare himself for a vocation; above all, he should so manage his life that the steps of his progress are taken without improper aids, that he calls no one master, that he does not win or deserve the reputation of being a tool of others, and that if called to public office he may assume its duties with the satisfaction of knowing that he is free to rise to the full height of his opportunity. If he can seek office without solicitations and promises, expressed or implied, which will interfere with the doing of his full duty, then he may seek with zest, and possibly he may find delight in the seeking. But I should rather say: Work in your chosen field to the best of your ability, enter into political activities without thought or demand of reward, do your duty as a citizen because it is your duty and not because you expect office, keep yourself free from embarrassing obligations, be ready to take office if it comes your way and you can take it; but never let the thought of your selection stay your efforts in aiding the community to better things.

The chief safeguard against inefficiency is accountability to the people. It is the fact of such accountability, under a proper system, which makes it possible to give adequate power to public officers. It is gratifying that there are so many evidences of a greater interest in administration and of increased determination to hold officers responsible for good work. The fact of accountability exists, but constant emphasis is needed as to what the people have a right to demand and for what they should hold their officers to account.

One fundamental difficulty in enforcing this accountability is found in the number of offices which are filled by election. As it has been thought necessary to protect the community against despotism by minute restrictions upon official authority, and by charters prolix with prohibitions, so it has also been thought necessary to multiply elective offices. In this the people have overshot the mark and defeated their own purpose. Accountability exists only in form if the attention of the people cannot be concentrated and their action pointed to the desired result. The distribution of official powers among a number of co-ordinate administrative officers, each elective, has the result that there is confusion as to the incidence of responsibility and frequently in popular understanding it is unjustly placed. In many of our States officers corresponding in their functions to members of the federal cabinet are elected by the people. Still, the governor as the executive head of the state is popularly regarded as charged with executive administration. It may be, however, that he has no real authority over the auditing department, as that may be in the hands of an elected comptroller. He may have no authority over the legal department, as that may be in the hands of an elected attorney-general. Frequently important public works are carried on under the supervision of elected boards, to which the executive head of the State may have slight relation or none at all. Thus executive responsibility is divided, and at the state elections a number of officers are chosen who in their separate spheres are quite as important as the chief executive in his sphere, while it is usually found that the attention of the people is concentrated upon the election of the latter, and comparatively slight attention is paid to the others.

A similar difficulty is found in municipalities. In many of our cities we have had almost a hopeless division of responsibility, so that it is difficult to lay defaults at any door. Such a system does not safeguard proper accountability and proceeds upon a mistaken theory.

The mistake is to suppose that the only method of enforcing accountability is to make an office elective. The centre of responsibility, of course, must be found in an elective office. But when such offices are made very numerous the result is that the people cling so tenaciously to a particular form that they lose the substance of their rights. They make it easy for cabals and machines to accomplish their purposes. These thrive on a multiplicity of elective offices which give them opportunities for combinations and manipulations which would otherwise be impossible. The remedy may be sought in a concentration of responsibility; in few offices and short ballots. The people will give their attention to the filling of an office in proportion to their conception of its dignity, of the importance of its work, of the extent of its responsibilities. The supposed danger from executive power and the range of executive discretion has its check in enlightened sentiment and short terms. A permanent service recruited on the basis of merit and fitness and so far as practicable through competitive examination; the grouping of administrative powers, with the necessary divisions or departments, under a chief administrative head; the enforcement of responsibility of the administrative head through an election upon which the attention of the people can be centred and with respect to the importance of which they are fully convinced, — in these, I believe, will be found important securities of efficient administration.

LECTURE III

POLITICAL PARTIES

"POPULAR government," says one of the keenest students of political institutions,[1] "especially as it approaches the democratic form, will tax to the utmost all the political sagacity and statesmanship of the world to keep it from misfortune." The able and sagacious men who laid the foundations of our institutions were as keenly alive to the dangers as to the advantages of popular rule, and they devoted their utmost effort to securing the expression of the will of the people through means which would aid the supremacy of wisdom and of virtue, and would guard against impatience and rash impulse. They chose the republican form of government with its representative feature, and confided administration "to a small number of citizens elected by the rest." In this they not only sought to provide a plan which would be workable over a vast extent of country, with a large population, but they were particularly anxious to furnish security against the mischiefs of party ambition and strife.

[1] Sir Henry S. Maine in "Popular Government."

Of these evils they were deeply sensible. And among the most important advantages of "a well constructed Union" they emphasize "its tendency to break and control the violence of faction." As Madison said: "The friend of popular governments never finds himself so much alarmed for their character and fate as when he contemplates their propensity to this dangerous vice." The words of Washington in his farewell address express a deep-seated conviction. The spirit of party, said he, "unfortunately is inseparable from our nature, having its root in the strongest passions of the human mind. It exists under different shapes in all governments, more or less stifled, controlled or repressed; but, in those of the popular form, it is seen in its greatest rankness, and is truly their worst enemy. The alternate domination of one faction over another, sharpened by the spirit of revenge, natural to party dissension, which in different ages and countries has perpetrated the most horrid enormities, is itself a frightful despotism."

It was the hope of the framers of the Constitution that they had constructed a system which would be unfavourable to party control and through which men would be selected to discharge the functions of government who would represent the larger interests of the Nation, unbiased by partisan animosities or by narrow considerations of party expediency. They expected "to refine and enlarge the public views, by passing them through the medium of a chosen body of citizens, whose wisdom may best discern the true interest of their country, and whose patriotism and love of justice will be least likely to sacrifice it to temporary or partial considerations."[1] They believed that as the sphere of government was extended they would enhance the protection against factious combinations, and that in a large republic such as the Union, they would find security by reason of the greater variety of parties and interests and of the difficulty of obtaining a majority of the same party.

But unwittingly they constructed a system, to the successful working of which parties were essential. That part of the system which, as Hamilton said, was almost the only part which escaped without severe censure from its opponents,[2] was the method of selecting the President. It was designed to have the immediate election made by a small number of men selected for the purpose who would be "most likely to possess the information and discernment" necessary for such a task. This plan

[1] The Federalist, No. 10.   [2] The Federalist, No. 68.

proved futile. The selection of the most important officer in the Nation could not be so far removed from popular choice. In the course of events it became manifest that the people were unwilling to confide to a body of electors chosen in the constitutional manner, the selection of a Chief Magistrate, and the electoral college has come to be simply a device for apportioning the popular vote for President and Vice-President according to States. But if the people were not content to turn over to a small number of men chosen within the respective States, the selection of a President, it was absolutely necessary that they should combine in groups to express their wishes with respect to candidates and policy. Not only is the spirit of party "inseparable from our nature," but the function of party has been found to be inseparable from our actual system of government. As President Lowell puts it: "The framers of the Constitution of the United States did not foresee the rôle that party was to play in popular government, and they made no provision for it in their plan; yet they established a system to which parties were a necessity. . . . If the electoral college was not really to select the President, it must become a mere machine for registering the results of a popular vote throughout the nation, and the candidates for the presidency must be designated beforehand in some way." [1]

The fact of main significance, however, is not that we have parties, not that they must be regarded as essential to the working of our government instead of being considered as evils, but that the tendency has been so marked to the establishment and continuance of two great parties which for the most part dominate the field of partisan activity. It was natural to suppose that the large variety of interests would be represented in numerous and changing groups or parties, and that no great party could maintain the solidarity requisite for long-continued effectiveness. Not only was the party coherence to which we are accustomed contrary to the expectations of the founders, but it has been a surprise to the modern critics of our institutions.

A great party must have its birth and grow its strength through political conviction. Where there is serious division among the people with respect to some fundamental question of national policy, or as to various related matters deemed to be of first importance, two great parties will reflect the

[1] In "The Government of England."

opposing views. The marvel is that when conditions change and major issues have been determined or cease to impress the popular imagination, when new conditions arise and unforeseen questions relating to new interests are presented, the former party divisions should continue to so great a degree unaltered.

The conflicting views with respect to the proper scope of national power, and the relation of the Nation to the States, which antedated the adoption of the Constitution, naturally furnished a line of division in the subsequent struggle between the Federalists and the Anti-Federalists. When the Republican party of Jefferson achieved supremacy, and the party of the Federalists bereft of leadership disappeared, there was for a time an absence of parties, properly speaking, and their place was taken by the rivalries of leaders and their personal followers. Great parties again developed in the Whigs and Democrats, which contested the field until the slavery issue forced a new alignment and the Republican party came into existence. Since, then, for upwards of fifty years, the two parties, Republican and Democratic, have maintained themselves as the great parties of the country, so far distancing all rivals in the extent of their popular support as to make other parties relatively insignificant.

This has been accomplished notwithstanding changes of extraordinary importance in our international position and in our internal conditions, and despite the rise of many new issues unforeseen fifty years ago. It exists despite the fact that in both the great parties there are views extremely divergent, and in one it may be said that there are antagonistic groups, each of which is further removed from the other in political theory than it is from the position of the great opposing party. Upon most of the great questions of the day, whether we have regard to the tariff, or to our financial system, or to the future of our insular possessions, or to foreign policy, or to the extension of the army and navy, or to the regulation of railroads and other public service corporations, or to the suppression of monopolistic combinations, it may fairly be supposed that were opinion freely expressed, the line of division would run across the great parties and not between them. The continued effectiveness of the great parties marks the recognition of the undesirability of the breaking up of party activities into those of small and ineffective groups, and a practical tendency to exercise the party function essential to the working of our government in a manner consistent with the concentration of controversy and the achievement substantially of majority rule.

While this demands suitable appreciation, it should not be over-emphasized. The absence of the unifying force of a paramount issue with respect to which the members of a great party are in accord, always threatens disintegration. There is danger in such case that in the course of events irreconcilable differences of opinion will achieve such importance that they will lead to the destruction of party unity and to the emergence of new groups or parties with their own candidates and policy. The counteracting influences, however, are very strong. There are the exigencies of opposition which require combination. There is an inherent disposition to oppose and to rally the forces of opposition under one banner upon the best available standing ground. Habit, tradition, and the sentiment of loyalty make their strong demands. There are, and probably always will be, small parties which are in effect parties of protest, content to adhere tenaciously to some principle without hope of temporary success, but with confidence in the unknown future. It is enormously difficult, however, to organize a great party. It must elicit a strong and widely diffused support and its birth must spring from a common conviction and from a general belief in its necessity. These conditions favour the subordination even of serious differences, and the maintenance of a fair degree of party solidarity. Disintegration might follow a success of one party so overwhelming as virtually to destroy all opposition, as was the case in the early part of the last century. And this would probably be followed, as then, by factional strife within the successful party and the formation of new parties. Or it might be that, as in the case of slavery, some great issue might arise, the force of which would destroy existing party lines and create new ones. Not improbably such an issue might be of a character which would tend to unite in opposition to each other the members of existing parties who are of conservative or radical tendencies respectively. But very likely we should still continue to have two great parties, even if names were different and constituencies were changed.

This concentration of political activity in two great parties has its obvious disadvantages. It would seem unfortunate to divide the people of a democracy into two hostile camps; to encourage habits of thought which engender prejudice and bitterness on the part of one-half of our citizens toward the other half; to accustom the people to regard public questions largely from the standpoint of partisan considerations rather than upon their individual merits; to make it difficult for those who belong to opposite parties to forward in an effective way some particular measure on which they are agreed; to divide the support of public officers who seek to secure the impartial administration of the public business; to make it difficult to present an issue to the people save through the devious methods of party politics and through the utterances of party platforms whose purposes so frequently are to conceal and to evade, in the interest of party expediency; to develop opportunities for chicanery and corruption, and to foster the designs of dishonourable and selfish political leaders who trade upon party loyalty.

But we cannot have the advantages of a situation without its disadvantages; and the former in this case greatly outweigh the latter. Division of political opinion is inevitable, and it will exist with regard to all public questions of importance. It is essential that there should be some means of focusing controversy and of providing a main line of division. If instead of two great parties we had a large number of little groups, each intent upon its own shibboleth and pressing its own candidates and policies, we should have a series of triumphant minorities, little or nothing would be settled, and the progress and prosperity which depend upon stability of government would be impossible. It should also be remembered that novel party proposals may be the fruit of long-forgotten seed, and that party action under changed conditions may simply reveal a tendency which earlier conditions with their dominant issues obscured. While the people are divided mainly into two parties, it is also true that in their general intercourse and through the organs of public opinion, particularly when there is no dominant issue, views are freely promulgated and a general sentiment is created which does not recognize the limitations of party boundaries. Such sentiment has its weight in party councils and much is accomplished through its existence, although it may not present an issue to be definitely passed upon in a political campaign. Through the instrumentalities of great parties the people generally do express what is uppermost in their minds. If there is some supreme issue actually engaging the thoughts of the people, in some way it will emerge and prove a decisive factor. The issue may not be that of the party platform; it may be more fundamental than that proposed by any particular propaganda. It may indeed merely involve a general attitude toward public questions and the sense of national security or insecurity under proposed leadership, or the desirability of continuity or change in administration with respect to its effect upon the prosperity of the country. Such judgments are really a popular synthesis of many public measures and proposals. The widening scope of national administration and the growing importance of the office of Chief Magistrate which represents the entire people and not simply a State or district, makes it of first consequence that candidacies should be limited, and that the President should rest his title upon a suffrage closely corresponding to an actual majority of the electorate. This can be accomplished only through great parties. It is not consonant with human nature that such parties should be expected suddenly to emerge and as quickly to disappear. Their tendency to continue reflects the conservatism of the people and the practicality in the conduct of government which gives assurance of permanence.

Parties, like the human society of which they form a part, resemble the flowing stream, continually changing, yet for long periods presenting the same appearance. The first voters at each presidential election are sufficient in numbers to alter the result in fairly close contests. Large numbers of voters hold their party ties very loosely and now vote with one party and now with another; and others, though originally they may have been strongly attached to one party, may find themselves for some time out of sympathy with its predominant sentiment, and hence gradually transfer their allegiance to the other. These adjustments are made without losing the advantage of maintaining two great parties in the field.

The realization of the desirability of having two great parties to focus our discussions in national affairs, and to make it possible to secure substantial majority rule, cannot but have an important effect on our individual party relations. I do not propose to discuss the history of the great parties, or their tenets or tendencies. It is the relation to party and not to the standards or the future of a particular party to which I desire to direct your attention.

In my judgment participation in the work of

one of the great parties offers an opportunity for service to the community, greater than that afforded by political activity outside them. In saying this I do not underestimate the public benefit derived from the action of those who are members of small parties or are entirely independent. Small parties by directing attention to matters of principle, sometimes by holding the balance of power in particular communities, exert an influence upon the action of great parties, even though they may not achieve directly any important success. They provide centres for the discussion upon their merits of topics of public interest, and their opportunites to bring forward candidates and policies and thus to test the state of public sentiment provide the community with important safety valves.

The influence exerted by men who are independent of party and vote solely with the purpose of supporting what they believe to be the best at the time, is of great value to the community. Uninfluenced by party tradition or ambition, they are a constant warning to party leaders and to faithless officials, and a stimulus to improved party methods. To a very important extent they furnish a natural corrective for unreasonable partisanship, and with unrestrained freedom of public expression they point with more or less impartiality to party failures and misdeeds, to the blunders or vices of leaders, and to the essentials of party success. Unmoved by mere considerations of party expediency, they almost unfailingly support administrative efforts which are for the general public interest, and they provide a basis for appeal over the heads of short-sighted party managers. Independence is of value in proportion to its militancy. This is achieved through the independent press, and its endeavours may be treated as representative; for it voices the sentiment of a constituency which is in sympathy with its general attitude and readily responds to its expressed opinions. And in so far as this constituency is earnest and measurably continuous it constitutes in effect a party with the principle of non-partisanship.

The regrettable feature of this non-relation to the great parties is that it withdraws from their active work men of weight and character who would be strongly influential in the determination of party action, and their withdrawal helps to create the conditions which they criticise. Not infrequently individual independence is a cover for disinclination to disagreeable and necessary work and shows a preference to stand aloof from the contests of democracy in which every citizen should take a vigorous part. This cannot be commended from any point of view. But the advantages flowing from the influence of conscientious independents, who seek nothing for themselves and strive earnestly to further what they believe to be for the best at the time should be recognized by every citizen, however strong his belief in the larger opportunity for service which affiliation with a great party affords.

What party a man shall join, or whether he shall join any party, is a question for his own conscience, and if he is upright and honourable in his conduct, and seeks justice in his decisions, he will be of public service. But the paradox is that the influence of the non-partisan who abhors party, must in the main be exercised through party. With respect to the choice of a President he must, if he counts at all, count with one of the great parties, and for the candidate of one or the other his vote must in effect be cast. Whatever his influence, it is likely to be the more potent because the more direct, if it is exercised within a party, as a recognized party member. However strong may be the sympathies of the individual, however intense his desire for capable and efficient government and for progress toward the attainment of democratic ideals, he must realize that this progress must be effected through the instrumentalities at our command. This does not imply that anyone of you should join a party contrary to your conscientious convictions; but in making up your mind as to what you should do, you should have a proper understanding of the means through which your influence as a citizen must be exercised, of the actual conduct of our affairs, and of the value of party relation. Independence has thrived on the stupidity, despotism, and corruption of party managers. It has performed notable services in voicing protest and in inflicting punishment. But we must still remember the actual necessities of the successful working of our system of government, and endeavour to put ourselves in such relation to the extraconstitutional machinery of the government, as to exercise to the fullest extent possible the privileges of our citizenship.

Belief in party, identification with one of the great parties, an intense desire to have it true to its best traditions and to enhance its public usefulness is not inconsistent with independence of character. Free expression of sentiment within the party, and forceful expression of conviction, whether or not it coincides with the wishes of the party managers, is essential to keep the party vigorous and wholesome. The spirit of faction, to advance personal interests, is hostile to party soundness and success; but so also is that sort of party harmony which is expressive of low ideals and the sway of repressive and despotic measures. The sincere party man will be as anxious to promote discussion, to foster the intelligent interest which springs from freedom of participation in party affairs, as he will be to end the unseemly clashes of personal ambitions. Party loyalty and patriotism should coincide, but if they are antagonistic, patriotism must ever be supreme. Important as it may be, the party is not the Nation or the State. He serves his party best who loves his country most. When, therefore, the temporary attitude of party threatens the interests of the community, when an ill-chosen policy invites general disaster, when party success means the debasement of the standards of honour and decency, the party man should recognize the superior obligation of his citizenship. We have no finer illustration of patriotic devotion than has been afforded by party men who at critical periods have deserted their party in order that they might serve the higher interests of their country and maintain the principles of administration which were essential to the common security. At times, not simply the interests of the people at large, but of the party itself, may justify the party man in acting independently of it. It is often the only available means of rebuke and of party discipline through which opportunity may be provided for a more healthful party life. The earnest party man will not find these occasions in personal disappointment or in slight dissatisfactions, nor will he be actuated by the spirit of revenge or lose sight of the need of party continuity and effectiveness. If intelligent and patriotic, he will endeavour to maintain a proper sense of proportion and to have his view of immediate duty conform to a true perspective, and his loyalty will be first to his country and next to his party's permanent interests.

I have thus far been speaking of national parties in their relation to national affairs. But the members of a national party, within their respective States, are citizens of the States. They not only vote every four years for President, but every two years within their congressional districts they vote for representatives in Congress. In these elections the issues are properly national. United States senators under the Constitution are elected by state legislatures, and where this function is discharged in fact and not merely as a matter of form pursuant to a popular vote for senators, the election of the members of the state legislature frequently has direct relation to national affairs. Moreover, the election of the administrative officers of the State, such as governor, lieutenant-governor, and attorney-general, is by the electorate of the entire State, and especially in the more populous States there is presented an exigency similar to that which we find in the Nation at large. To limit candidacies and to focus discussion, party action is advisable, and state issues separately considered have not been so sharply defined as generally to call into existence, much less to maintain, great state parties as distinguished from those in the national field. In these conditions, it is inevitable that national parties should take part in state elections, and they have served to perform the party function with respect to the affairs of the States. The moral influence of party successes in state elections cannot be overlooked, for the disposition of the people to act in state matters according to their affiliations with national parties is deemed to give to the result of their action a national significance.

The actual administration of state affairs, however, rarely has any close connection with questions of national concern. A state governor may perform his duties for years without being called upon to deal in his official capacity with any question that may fairly be called national. And as the people become interested in state affairs, and local questions achieve prominence in their minds, independence tends to increase. They show a growing disposition to refuse to be influenced by the appeals of the national party to which they belong, and for local reasons to choose to state offices men of opposite national faith. The election, three times in succession, of Governor Johnson, a Democrat, in a state strongly Republican, is an illustration, and others are not lacking where the support of state governors to a considerable extent has been composed of men of all parties whose action with respect to state issues does not imply surrender of their party convictions or their national party relations. It cannot be doubted that this tendency to break away from national parties in state elections is deplored by the leaders of the national parties, or rather by those of the party which suffers the loss, as it is deemed to imperil the party integrity. These fears are often exaggerated as the voters show increasing capacity to discriminate between those elections in which really they are dealing with national issues, and those in which they are not. However, the national parties are in the field and it is not likely that permanent parties of a separate character will be formed to discharge the party function in the State. More probable is it that the national parties will seek to meet the exigencies of state issues by presenting candidates selected with due regard to such issues, and that the immediate demands which may not be satisfied in this way will be met by independent voting or by independent nominations.

Divisions according to national party lines extend beyond the state elections to the local elections in counties and cities. Here we are removed from considerations which are germane to national controversies, and questions are presented which require an examination of the nature and tendencies of party organization.

Every party to be effective must be organized. Whether loose or systematic in its internal arrangement, it must in some way provide its councils, its representatives, its organs of expression. Condemnation of party organization, as such, is absurd. If it be deemed important that we should have great national parties, in order to concentrate political discussions, and to make political controversies suitably serve their purpose by having decisions made, so near as may be, by a majority of a vast electorate, it is likewise important that these parties be properly organized and managed. It is true that the need of precise and detailed organization is in inverse ratio to the intensity of party conviction. When national party feeling is intense with regard to some great issue, campaigns almost manage themselves. Every voter, alive with interest, is in some degree a campaign manager; discussions are spontaneous; the public feeling is manifested in frequent demonstrations; every gathering is a political meeting. Great as may be the value even in such cases of orderly management, the need of prearrangement is slight compared with that in listless campaigns. The vote comes without coaxing.

This is well illustrated in the description which Carl Schurz gives of Lincoln's first campaign for the presidency. He says: "The campaign was hardly opened when the whole North seemed to get into commotion. It looked as if people, especially in the smaller cities and towns and the country districts, had little else to do than to attend meetings, listen to speeches, march in processions, and carry torches after nightfall. 'Wide-Awake' companies with their glazed capes and caps, the prototypes of the modern marching clubs of party organizations, sprang up all over the land as by magic. Brass bands, some of them very trying to musical ears, seemed to grow out of the earth. And all this was done without any official machinery, for the postmasters and revenue officers, and district attorneys and United States marshals with their retinues were on the Democratic side. The Republicans held only a few State and municipal offices, hardly worth mentioning as political agencies. Nor was there much money used in stirring and keeping up the agitation. The funds at the disposal of the Republican National Committee were beggarly compared with the immense sums that nowadays flow into the war chests of such bodies. The State and local committees were generally in the same condition. In a large measure the campaign seemed to run itself. It was not necessary to drum up audiences for meetings by extraordinary tricks of advertising or of alluring attractions. The simplest notice sufficed to draw a crowd. Not seldom large gatherings were altogether extemporized."

But when party spirit languishes, when many are indifferent, when the importance of the nature of the issues may not be apprehended, then the most careful management is required and less reliance can be placed upon the spontaneity of the party members. It is also natural that national parties should reflect, as they do reflect, the talent for organization of the American people. It is a common saying with us that political activities do not engage men of the highest order of ability; that citizens of conspicuous attainments are not found in the work of political management. It is customary to decry politicians generally, not simply because of supposed motive, but as being men of inferior talent. While it is doubtless true that many men of distinguished eminence in various lines of effort abstain from participation in political affairs, it is idle to ignore the fact that a large part of the ability of the country is devoted to political activity. In national affairs and in our States the record of men of eminent talent would be conspicuously deficient if it did not include the names of those who had largely made political effort the field for display of their skill and astuteness. In the State of New York, for example, a large number of the greatest names of history are those of political leaders who were none the less politicians because now, being dead, they are styled statesmen. It is true that the growth of cities and of the relative importance of local organizations, and the conditions in which they work, has tended seriously to impair the quality and ability of political leadership. But although exercised to so large an extent on a low plane, conspicuous ability in organization and management is continually manifested. It must be recognized that the development of political machinery during recent decades is a striking illustration of the tendency to thorough organization with respect to matters in which a deep interest is taken and which provide opportunities for the play of individual talent.

We find party organization to be essential, and in its main purpose desirable. If to-day the purest-minded men in the country were to combine in a political party to further the noblest cause, they would proceed to effect the best organization which they could devise, with leaders of tens and cap-

IN DEMOCRATIC GOVERNMENT

tains of hundreds, with companies, battalions, and regiments, whom they would seek to inspire with loyalty to the common purpose, and upon whose efficient and united work they would rely for its accomplishment. This would simply be an effort at effective co-operation. It would be favoured by our modern facilities of intercourse and the rapidity of communication. It would be justified by its motive, and many who had been loudest in the condemnation of "machines" would be conspicuous within its ranks. Sometimes the extreme of personal domination is found in organizations most severe in denunciation of machine methods.

I shall not undertake to describe the form of party organization. It varies with respect to certain details in different States and in different communities in the same State. But the differences are inconsequential. The essence of the matter is that there shall be party representatives, committees, and executive heads, according to appropriate political units, and that these shall work in harmony as a part of a general scheme of organization. And so far as it is truly representative, so far as through it the wishes of the members of the party find genuine expression and the organization performs its proper function within its legitimate field, there is no ground for just criticism. There must be methods by which party candidates may be selected, policies announced, campaigns managed, and proper efforts directed to the bringing out of the full party strength at the polls.

In these activities it is important that the standards of true political leadership should be clearly perceived and constantly maintained. Party leaders in the higher sense must be distinguished from those party managers who are confined to the narrow range of the activities of small districts, and hence seldom get a wide horizon or a true perspective. But management on a large scale, with regard to the exigencies of extended communities, should develop political leadership of a high order; and whether the field be great or small, party management should be infused with the spirit and devoted to the aims of such leadership within its sphere.

The true political leader must be a man of sympathy and quick perception. He should have political insight and foresight. He must be swift to detect the movement of public opinion and the exigencies of conditions. He should understand how to relate the prior action of his party to the next appropriate step in the line of its general policy which will commend the party to public approval and justify continued confidence. He should not wait to be driven by public indignation. In the forwarding of measures or the shaping of issues he should never forget that the final test will be the public interest, and that while he may move within the broad limits assigned to him by the traditions of his party, public service must ever be the highest party expediency and that public injury is an ineffaceable stain upon the party record. He must be a good judge of men so that those whom he favours as the candidates of his party for public place shall exhibit integrity and eminent qualifications. Able administration is a party asset of high value. With respect to the management of campaigns he must have not only executive skill and capacity for the mastery of detail, but he must also be able to inspire zeal, to exact fidelity, and to win confidence in his leadership. He must have precise information as to conditions within his sphere of work and exhibit the industry and pertinacity which are essential to success in every effort. It may be rare that any one man should display all these characteristics. The field is wide and the labourers are many, but the ideals of leadership should always be kept in view.

Whatever his astuteness, his knowledge, or his political sagacity, it is essential to the proper representation of his party that he should be a man of honour, of integrity, and should be unselfish in his work. The moment he puts the maintenance of his personal power ahead of the party interests, or endeavours, through his activities as a party leader, to fill his own pocket, he is a traitor to his cause and deserves not only the scorn of all honest men, but particularly contemptuous repudiation by the party which he has betrayed.

Above all, the true party leader should recognize that he is a leader and not the master of his party. He should always be content to abide by the uncoerced, unintimidated, and unbought suffrage of the party members, and should seek to support himself by candour with respect to issues and candidates and by honourable management, and when his appeal to his constituency fails he should be willing and desirous to step down.

Now it may be said that this is a counsel of perfection. Certainly it is too much to expect that we shall have angels or archangels in political work when they are found nowhere else. But as we have party organization, as it is not to be abolished but springs from manifest necessities, the proper conditions and qualities of leadership should be recognized. As in our colleges to-day are doubtless many of the political leaders of the future, here we should expect, if anywhere, the standards of public morality and honour to be set up, and those who enter political life should understand that they do not thereby receive indulgences to commit iniquity, but assume obligations of the highest importance to the public which the advantages of training, of broad outlook, and of inspirational associations should in an eminent degree qualify them to discharge.

LECTURE IV

POLITICAL PARTIES (*Continued*)

As self-discipline draws the line in individual conduct between use and abuse, and the wise man is the one who knows where to draw it, so in the self-discipline of democracy we must be alive to the abuses of party organization. These abuses tend to corrupt the very core of government and the intelligent citizen should not only be severe in denouncing them, but most solicitous to apprehend their causes and the most practicable methods by which, in any important degree, they may be corrected.

Party organization for the benefit of party is one thing; party organization for the benefit of party managers and party workers is quite another. The degeneracy of the former into the latter is most natural and is due to the working of self-interest in circumstances of peculiar opportunity. It is natural that those whose main business is to maintain party solidarity should concern themselves chiefly with the interests of a phalanx of voters upon whose fidelity they can absolutely depend. The constant association of the members of these groups with their exclusively partisan outlook tends to deaden the sensibility to those political tendencies which are more largely reflected in independent opinion. The blindness of those who make a business of politics is frequently amazing. They learn too late and the lessons even of condign punishment are soon forgotten. They rarely appreciate their own standing in public estimate. This is not due to lack of native ability or of skill in certain methods of management, but is largely the result of their own close occupation with the baser and more sordid motives of political action. The conditions of his work are such as largely to hinder the political manager from taking broad and statesmanlike views. He is constantly subject to most seductive influences and to interested importunities; he is handicapped by faulty traditions and not infrequently he regards himself as constrained by supposed political necessities and by the like or worse conduct of rivals.

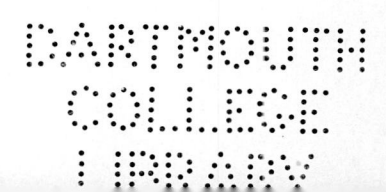

The party is supposed to exist for the sake of principles, and in our national campaigns these principles, so far as there are such, are bound to come to the front. Party managers, in theory, are supposed to devote themselves to the party in order that its principles may be advanced and thereby the community be served. But party organization demands work and a corps of workers. The effective political machine consists not of inanimate parts, but of men variously related to the common effort, giving largely of their time and in many cases of their money in political work. The conduct of campaigns entails an immense amount of labour, and between campaigns the organization must be kept up, party questions discussed, and the interest and alignment of voters maintained. The average American of aptitude is busy. He supports himself by his own labour. The demands upon his energies in the maintenance of his family or in the advancement of his business or professional interests are insistent. The American slogan is "hustle." The prizes of life go to those who put their whole soul into their chosen pursuit. The political leader is faced with the necessity of procuring workers. He must have men at his call; the better the class of work he wants, the harder it is to get it without paying for it in some way. This is particularly true when there is no deep feeling with regard to issues and assistance is not freely offered. In order to make a

IN DEMOCRATIC GOVERNMENT 93

man of much use in the practical affairs of politics, he must know the men with whom he deals. Continuity in political work is important political capital, because of the intimate knowledge of men and relations which it brings. The party manager desires constantly to maintain an effective force of men of political experience who have been through former contests. How is such a force to be kept in the field? For its support the manager naturally comes to look to the public treasury. It is little short of inevitable that he should seek to quarter his army upon the people at large. If rewards are to be given, from what source shall they so easily come as through the opportunities of public place? But the party manager needs more than men. He must have money in order that men may work effectively. The more thoroughly campaigns are managed, the more expensive they become. The cost of mere spectacular demonstration is itself large, but that of holding meetings for public discussion, of providing speakers, of circulating political "literature," and of publishing advertisements is enormous. The expense of placing one circular in the hands of every voter in the State of New York is probably upwards of $25,000. In educational campaigns the limit of the outlay would seem to be only in the amount that can be raised. In order to provide this money, subscriptions are freely asked, but the manager naturally desires as many large contributions as he can possibly obtain. His best source of supply under former laws was from the treasury of large corporations, in whose accounts the payments could easily be buried in unmarked graves. Corporations holding enormous accumulations for the benefit of numerous persons, such as insurance companies for example, found it very easy to make political contributions to advance the political opinions of those in charge. This practice has been the means of blackmail and corruption. Interests which may be the subject of legislation, or are under the supervision of departments, do not wish by refusal to incur enmity; or they may desire to purchase immunity or favour. The necessity of raising the necessary moneys for legitimate campaign expenditures at once puts the political manager in an equivocal position and makes him the instrument of solicitation and of promise. But the worst is yet to be said, for he finds himself in a condition where, to justify his leadership, he feels that he must control the vote of the venal and corrupt. His conscience tends to become honeycombed by the traditions of his work; he sees so many votes which he thinks can be had only by buying them, and which, if he does not buy them, will be bought by his opponents. To him political morality is a dream of those who know nothing of the necessity of "getting out the vote" on election day and thus swelling the total to which statesmen may point with pride. So he buys votes or winks at bribery, either lamenting the necessity, or too often devoting his skill to the enlargement of the nefarious traffic.

The creed of the party manager is ordinarily very simple. To him, as a rule, public office is an organization trust. According to this view no one should be put forward as a candidate of the party who will not "recognize" the party organization; that is, who will not, in making his appointments, select the men whom the organization desires to be selected. A candidate for nomination who it is feared will be independent in his selections will not be permitted to succeed if the party managers can compass his defeat without a dangerous irritation of public feeling. In an ideal condition from the organization standpoint, the party managers, or in a single district the local manager, would select all the appointees of the elected officer, and the latter would simply carry out his instructions. The condition would be deemed tolerable if the elected officer, desirous of some latitude of choice, were willing to make the selections from a list furnished to him by the managers. It would frequently answer the purpose if in case the elected officer had decided objections to the persons recommended, he were to request other recommendations and finally make a selection which would be mutually satisfactory. This would probably suffice unless the party manager or managers were for some reason especially interested in a particular applicant and determined that he should have the place; in that case the refusal of the elected officer to make the desired appointment upon the ground that he wished to make his own selection, would be regarded in diplomatic language as "unfriendly," or if it were supposed to indicate a line of policy would not improbably be considered as an unpardonable affront. If the purpose of the officer were believed to be to displace the party manager or to increase his own power within the party machine, his course would be vigorously antagonized; yet, as being more consistent with time-honoured practice in contests for political control, it would more likely be condoned than if he were simply to assert his independence of the organization in order that he might by free selection according to his own judgment better discharge his constitutional functions. In the latter case even his party standing might be called in question.

It should not be understood that the purpose of the organization in controlling appointments is to put bad men in office, or men who are incapable of performing its duties. It is generally sought to supply a man who, although he is not conspicuously fit, is deemed by the organization to be good enough for the place. The primary purpose is to provide an office for a party worker either simply as a reward for what he may have done in party service, or to furnish a base of supply which will support him in further party activity. Exceptional conditions may from time to time arise in which either by reason of the special demands of the places to be filled or of the state of public sentiment, it may be recognized by the party managers as advisable that the selection should be made outside the lines generally laid down. But such an exigency is most unwelcome. In the view of the organization the successful candidate owes his success to its efforts; party work cannot be effectively done unless public places to a large extent are provided for those who do the work; promises, express or implied, made in the course of the campaign must be redeemed; the party organization must be recognized as the supreme party authority, carrying with it the control of patronage, and hence the elected officer who refuses to act within these limitations is regarded not only as ungrateful, but as acting in hostility to his party's interests.

The injury to the public service that is inflicted by the subordination of public officers to such control is obvious. Administrative efficiency is made difficult if not impossible. However strongly it may be claimed that it is only desired to put men in office who have decent qualifications, the tendency manifestly is to a low level of public work. The standards of efficiency are bent to the demands of favour. The aim is not to get the best, but to pay for party work and support the party worker. The party manager is under the pressure of constant solicitation; he is burdened with the obligations of campaigns; and however good his general intention he cannot be expected to resist the temptation to put inferior men upon the public pay-roll. Incumbents regard their places as held not by virtue of the public service they give, but by the grace of the managers they have served and continue to serve. It cannot be supposed that as a rule public work can be performed in the manner in which it ought to be performed if places are parcelled out to meet the exigencies of political management, or through a system by which elected officers act under the dictation of those who have not been chosen to exercise official responsibilities. Exceptions undoubtedly may be found in communities where political managers are astute enough to require a fair degree of efficiency and at the same time (which is the most important) are strong enough to resist the appeals of the unworthy; but these exceptions are so rare as to prove the general tendency.

Even as I write these words, confirmation comes in the report which has been made to Congress by the Secretary of the Treasury. Speaking of the scandal recently disclosed in the customs service, one of the worst scandals of this generation, Mr. MacVeagh says: "The study of the causes of the demoralization which has been revealed is still incomplete, but the main causes are evident. It is clear, for instance, that the influence of local politics and politicians upon the customs service has been most deleterious, and has promoted that laxity and low tone which prepare and furnish an inviting soil for dishonesty and fraud. Unless the customs service can be released from the payment of political debts and exactions, and from meeting the supposed exigencies of political organization, big and little, it will be impossible to have an honest service for any length of time. Any considerable share of the present cost of this demoralization to the public revenues, to the efficiency of the service, and to public and private morality, is a tremendous amount to pay in mere liquidation of the small debts of political leaders."

We have not simply to consider the demands of organization working for the benefit of party. Commingled with these demands are the personal requirements of party managers eager to maintain their own power. They must have not only an army of party adherents, but each party manager requires personal adherents pledged to his individual fortunes, who realize that they stand or fall, not simply with the success or defeat of the party, but with the continuance or loss by the party manager of the control of his district. Thus we have not only party machines, but personal machines, using party names and appealing to party loyalty, although the party interest may be a secondary consideration. The feudal system again appears with its lord, his vassals and retainers, and the common tillers of the political soil. Within his district the manager needs the offices to enforce his personal authority and distribute his personal rewards; he dictates nominations; elections are won through the organized support that he furnishes; the elected officers obey his will in making appointments; and the administration of government is within his control. He maintains himself in a citadel fortified by the public purse. It is extremely difficult to depose him, not only because of the abundant means at his command, but frequently also by reason of the complicated system of organization and of the methods of selecting candidates which favour the perpetuation of power. The city affords the greatest opportunities for the development of such autocracy, because of the extent of available patronage, the compactness of the population, and the elements of which it is composed. In the full play of his influence, when commanding those whom he has placed in official position, he becomes mayor, common council, commissioner of public works, head of the police department, as well as sheriff and district attorney. When challenged he calls himself "the organization." If astute to avoid an uprising through outraged public sentiment, he will endeavour to give a semblance of efficient government and may indeed provide it with respect to many functions of administration. He will not, if skilful, interfere unnecessarily with the ordinary processes of government; he will be content to hold his army together and only upon occasion to impose his commands. But when he interferes his word is law. Generally in the city he will regard the control of the police as most important. For the granting of indulgences to law-breakers and the tempering of police authority by his discretion are among the main, though secret, sources of his strength.

Thus is created an irresponsible personal government not only unknown to the Constitution, but alike unknown to any admissible theory of government by party. This is the government of the so-called "boss." Men of this type differ in respect of ability and intelligence. Some may have a large outlook upon public affairs and seek the support of disinterested and public-spirited citizens by frequent use of their power to public advantage. Others may be cynical or even brutal. They invariably invoke the party tradition and appeal to party "regularity." But the "boss" displays the same characteristics in whatever party we find him. One party flag may fly in one community, and another in another; but they cover the same sinister designs. If they are threatened by public measures, or legislation is aimed at evils which thrive under their protection, they unite and the divisions of party are forgotten in the defence of the common cause. They soon aspire to influence beyond the limits of their districts. They control the nomination of members of the Legislature and dictate their votes upon legislative measures. If the latter disobey they are left at home; their humiliation gives no concern; it is the just punishment of treason. The presence in a State of a number of local managers enjoying power in communities of large population, leads to the effort to create definite spheres of admitted influence and a division of state patronage for the purpose of assigning to one or more control over state functions similar to that which is exercised locally in a city or county. Between them, these managers may largely or altogether, according to the measure of success they attain, dominate a state legislature and state officers.

I trust I have made it plain that not every party

manager becomes a "boss." On the contrary, in many communities party managers have neither the opportunity, the aptitude, nor the purpose to achieve such distinction. They are content with a more restricted sphere of party activity and exercise their influence along lines which, while true to the ideals of party organization, do not aim at the domination of government through personal machines.

But the abuses of party organization are fraught with other dangers than those which involve the impairment of public service and the maintenance of the personal rule of the "boss." There is a constant effort by special interests to shape or to defeat legislation, to seek privileges, and to obtain favours in the administration of departments. So close is the relation of government to many large enterprises, particularly to public service corporations, that there is the strongest incentive to control the government in their interest. For this purpose they are willing to supply the sinews of political campaigns and desire in return to name legislators and administrative officers. The political machine, especially the personal machine, furnishes the most ready instrument to their purpose. The result is the making of corrupt alliances between party managers and special interests, the former eager for power and money, the latter seeking protection and governmental favouritism. In these alliances we have the most dangerous conspiracy against the government of the Nation, the State, and the local community.

Apology is sometimes made for these methods as necessary for the protection of enterprises against reckless and blackmailing assault. But is it not better to rely upon open argument and fair discussion of the requirements of legitimate enterprise than to seek protection in the corruption of government and thus to arouse public indignation and widespread resentment? The security of business in this country cannot depend upon the debauching of legislators and the perverting of administration. The final foundation of successful enterprise must be found in integrity and respect for law, and cannot securely rest upon the dishonour of our institutions. The more important the undertakings of business, the more essential is it that they should find support in the just appreciation of a contented people. Shall not our intelligent men of business learn the lesson, "Whatsoever ye sow, that shall ye also reap"?

The importance of party organization is too

great, and its perversion is too serious a menace to permit us to be content with mere adjuration to political managers or to those who seek protection or profit in their power. But what remedies are available? Certainly human nature will not change. The political field offers the widest opportunity for the exhibition of its infirmities, and we shall continue to see the play of avarice and ambition, the schemes of selfishness and the machinations of unscrupulous cunning seeking to convert to their purpose institutions however essential, and methods of co-operation however well designed. The course of progress lies between the fanciful schemes of those who ignore the actual components of society and its mixed qualities, and the let-alone policy supported alike by the indifferent, the cynical, and those who despair of improvement. That we cannot accomplish everything is no reason why we should not attempt anything; and with patience and a firm determination that cannot be shaken by ridicule, rebuff, or temporary defeat, we should seek that immediate gain and the next practicable advance which our judgment may approve. This is to play our part according to our light and opportunity in the long struggle which has brought us the advantages of this favoured day and the issue of which in our time will make for the happiness or the misfortune of the coming generations.

No remedy is possible which does not have its roots in general sentiment, and in large degree the remedial agencies must be those exclusively of public opinion. Here and there, of course, opinion may best accomplish its purpose through legal enactment. But tradition and common conviction are frequently better than law and accomplish results which by reason of its necessary limitations the law cannot reach. We have already noted the advantages of having two great parties in the national field. Whatever is attempted must be consistent with party activity and the maintenance of national party organizations. They are none the less inevitable, and none the less desirable, because they may be characterized as machines. The loosening of party ties and the separation of men of public spirit from party activities withdraws the beneficial efforts of those who would aid in maintaining proper standards of party work, and tends to make easier the control of those who profit by its abuse. What then is admissible which will not improperly cripple efficiency of national parties?

The fact that the great parties are national,

suggests at once their appropriate field, and the evils that exist point clearly to the conclusion that very largely they are due to the extension of the work of these parties into spheres to which they have no legitimate relation. We may therefore accomplish much by seeking to limit their activity to what properly belongs to them, and thus to narrow the range of appeals to party loyalty where party concerns are not involved, and of opportunities to convert party loyalty inspired by national ideals to the personal advantage of party workers.

For example, there is the matter of judicial elections. There is a growing demand that our judges should be taken out of party politics. This is reflected in the tendency to demand that a judge who has served faithfully should be renominated by both the great parties without regard to his party affiliations. The non-partisan quality of judicial work should be recognized in original nominations as well as in renominations. It is evident that this is in process of accomplishment. Where judges are appointed, this tendency is shown from time to time in the appointment of men of the minority party, or in a balancing of appointments so as to achieve something like non-partisanship through bi-partisanship. Judges should be chosen by reason of their fitness for the judicial office in point of ability, integrity, and professional qualifications. This office is the last place that should be used for the purpose of party rewards. In communities where judges are elected, tradition has long accustomed us to the nomination of judges by political parties, and wherever the sentiment is such that party nominations are likely to meet with favour, undoubtedly they will continue to be made. But all efforts to submerge party considerations in the choice of candidates, to facilitate independent choices, to rebuke the use of judgeships as a part of party patronage, should be encouraged by the public-spirited citizen. No one should be expected as a faithful party man to support the candidate of his party for a judgeship merely because he is the candidate of his party. The sentiment should be encouraged that loyalty to national parties demands no such support, and that without loss of party standing men may vote for judges according to their views of personal fitness. As this sentiment develops, party nominations, where they are made, will become more and more a formal method of expressing a sentiment which is not confined to party lines. Ultimately we may be able entirely to dissociate judicial elections from national party considerations, and any practicable measure to this end should be adopted. But meanwhile the most forceful influence will be the extending conviction that national party obligations are released when judges are to be chosen.

I trust the same will be true of prosecuting attorneys. The prosecution of offenders on behalf of the State and the quasi-judicial functions of the office should be removed from the field of party politics. This in time may also come to be recognized in the case of the administrative officers of counties. Sheriffs, county clerks, boards of supervisors, and district attorneys have no legitimate relation to national concerns. Public sentiment in most of our communities is yet far short of this view. But we may look forward with some degree of confidence to the time when citizens of counties will select their administrative representatives and their prosecuting officer without any sense of control or duty by reason of their relation to national parties. Those who think that this will impair the efficiency of national parties are intent upon maintaining sources of patronage despite all the evils that flow from its use for party purposes. They conceive that national party organization, with its local divisions, requires an alignment with regard to matters of purely local concern. But this misconception of the field of national parties, while persistent, may yet yield to a truer appreciation of civic relations. For while the present methods may tend to provide sustenance for party organization, they also over-develop it by giving it opportunities which it has no right to demand, thereby entailing abuses which could largely be removed if local sentiment enforced a proper restriction.

Of even greater importance is the limitation of the influence of national parties with respect to the election of officers of cities. Municipal government has put democracy to the blush and we have been disgraced by the inefficiency and corruption displayed in its administration. It would seem that capacity for self-government would be best shown in local affairs, particularly in those of great communities, because of the close relation of administration to the daily concerns of the people. It would be expected that these interests, together with the pride of local citizenship, would elicit the most active efforts for economy and intelligent management. Instead, we find the greatest waste, the most inexcusable shiftlessness, and the most corrupting agencies in connection with municipal enterprise.

It cannot be doubted that the intrusion of national party politics, with the divisions and cohesions caused by national party loyalties, into the affairs of cities is largely responsible for this. Their exigencies have furnished the basis for local organization with the control of the city government as its primary object. Such are the opportunities of local administration that these associations come to be mere combinations for the enrichment of their more powerful members. Concern for the national interests of the party are subordinated to the greed of municipal parasites. Whenever such a combination exists for the dominating, not to say looting, of a city, the first duty of the citizens is to demolish it, whatever party name it bears. The movement in this direction is making gratifying progress throughout the country.

That municipal elections have nothing to do with national politics was recognized in effect by the amendment to the Constitution of the State of New York in 1894, which provided for separate municipal elections to be had in odd-numbered years. In the constitutional convention its president, Joseph H. Choate, tersely expressed the sentiment which underlay the proposal, when he said: "There is no reason why a man should be mayor of New York simply because he is a Republican or because he is a Democrat, or that any other municipal office should be filled by this man or the other because he belongs to one national party or the other. The questions of national and state politics have nothing to do with the honest, expedient, and prudent administration of municipal affairs."

The problems of municipal administration have long engaged the attention of thoughtful students of our political life, and this study is bearing fruit in recent experiments. The adoption here and there of new methods of city government and for the nomination of city officers, the tendency of citizens to combine irrespective of national parties in choosing city officers, and the growing emphasis placed upon the importance of concentration of administrative responsibility, attest the rising demand that organizations of national parties shall not be permitted to control city politics. We cannot tell what may be the result of the experiments now being tried and it is not possible here to discuss their individual merits. But it would seem that national party nominations for municipal offices will be held in growing disfavour, and that in time party nominations as such will be denied a place upon official ballots. Other means will be devised for expressing the will of the citizens with respect to their local interests, quite apart from their views upon national matters. Where the sentiment supporting the activity in local affairs of national party organizations continues to be strong, their tickets will be placed in the field, and proposals to eliminate them altogether will not be successful. But the criticism of this activity will probably increase, and the disposition to join with others in so-called non-partisan or independent movements and thus to cloak the unwarrantable intrusion of a national party into civic affairs will become stronger. The aim should be to cultivate such an appreciation of civic obligation, and of the proper sphere of the efforts of national parties, that an independent attitude with respect to the selection of city officers will come to be recognized as the normal and fitting attitude, and that the nominations by national parties as such for city offices will no longer find place in the political scheme.

Freeing our cities from the control of national party organizations, and the development of a

IN DEMOCRATIC GOVERNMENT 115

system of local government which will aid in concentrating administrative responsibility, will remove many of the most pernicious abuses. This will not interfere with the proper function of these organizations. They will still exist for national purposes; and all the legitimate exigencies of national parties may still be met. The local "boss," however, will largely lose his patronage, and the conditions will tend to favour organization for the benefit of party under suitable leadership, rather than personal machines constructed and equipped to prey upon local enterprise. So long as national party tickets are presented in any community, and in whatever field its efforts may be exerted, it is of the highest importance that the organization should be as representative as possible. With respect to candidates, members of party committees, and campaign managers, it should represent the will of the party voters. Where methods exist through which nominations made on behalf of party members are virtually dictated by party managers, and party committees and managers are thus aided in perpetuating their control, they should be changed so as to improve the opportunities and thus safeguard the rights of the party voters. I believe that the selection of party candidates directly by a secret official ballot cast by properly enrolled members of the party, and the direct election in a similar manner of members of party committees, will be an important protection against the abuses arising from those defects in machinery which prove the obstacles to the effective expression of the wishes of the party voters and make it easy for managers to entrench themselves in power. There is no reason why this should not be accomplished through provisions which will not fail to recognize the value of the advice and suggestions of party representatives elected by the party members to positions of responsibility. To place the ultimate right of choice both of party officers and of candidates for office with the party voters themselves, thus giving the ordinary men who cannot make politics a business an opportunity to participate effectively in the affairs of his party, will, I believe, prove a valuable obstacle to the development of despotic power and to the misuse of party organization in the interest of corrupt alliances.

The further extension of the practice of filling subordinate places through competitive examinations is another important means of remedying the abuses that have existed. It is easy to ridicule this sort of test, but it affords a far better method of selection than is employed in the use of patronage as rewards for party services. The shaping of examinations so as to develop the qualifications of the candidate, or his lack of them, with reference to the particular office is a matter requiring close attention and the utmost care in administration. In the course of experience we find abundant reason for extending the use of civil service examinations; their propriety becomes apparent with respect to positions which formerly it was thought best to exempt; and the tendency is to limit the opportunities of those who would use offices as the spoils of party victories. This tendency should be encouraged, and it is gratifying to find that officers who desire to equip their departments on the basis of efficiency, although at first somewhat restive under the restraints of civil service rules, learn to appreciate their advantage and to give the merit system their cordial support. The chief administrative places, which remain exempt from competitive examination, will continue to be the object of the pursuit of those who wish to use them for party advantage. Against this effort we must rely upon intelligent public opinion forcing upon the appointing officer the conviction that he will be held strictly accountable for the use of the appointing power so as to secure the best available service for the State.

I have already spoken to you upon the paramount importance of administrative efficiency in view of the expanding operations of government. The appreciation of this by the people inevitably will lead to the selection of public officers who will feel their responsibility and will resist in greater degree improper importunities. There can be no doubt that the people desire to see public officers perform their constitutional duties of administration according to their conscience and best judgment. Divided as the people are, for the most part, into two great parties, still there is abundant evidence that they do not desire that the officers they elect should be controlled by party machines in the administration of the public business. Their support of efforts which they believe to be in the public interest is a lesson to those who would make party organization a vehicle of public mischief. And the people have too much common sense not to recognize that insistence upon impartial and capable administration is not incompatible with earnest devotion to the interests of the national parties, but should be, as indeed they profess it to be, the ideal of both.

There has been much legislation of late for the purpose of restricting some of the evils we have noted. In some jurisdictions corporations have been prohibited from making contributions to campaign funds. Such contributions are utterly indefensible. If they are made to secure immunity or to gain favour for special interests, they are an offence to public morals. If they are made simply to reflect the political opinions of executive officers, they are a violation of trust. Provision has also been made to secure publicity of campaign contributions and to guard against corrupt practices. Political committees are required to file reports of their receipts and expenditures. The working of these statutes in practice must constantly be observed in order that they may be perfected to prevent evasion. And experience will doubtless show the way to additional precautions in the protection of the purity of the ballot. Of great importance also will be the movement to which I have already alluded in the direction of reducing the number of elective offices and providing simple and short ballots. The advantage of many other proposals of improved methods will turn largely upon the facility with which public opinion can be concentrated and the wishes of the voters expressed. So long as we have national party tickets in local elections it is most desirable that straight party voting should not be favoured, and that ballots should be so arranged as to require a statement of the voter's preference for each office.

The perversion of party organization prospers through ignorance, indifference, and cupidity. Against the first we must rally the forces of education; not simply instruction in the elementary branches, in science, general history, language, and literature, but in the actual operations of our government. Nor is ignorance to be looked for exclusively among the poor and lowly, or in the congested settlements of great cities. The knowledge of those who have been deprived of the higher advantages of education, with respect to the actual working of government, often puts to the blush many favoured sons of our higher schools. We need constantly to deal with the facts of our governmental system and these should be estimated at a higher degree of importance than the mere learning of dates of battles, or of the birth and succession of kings. The first object of the citizen of a free community should be to understand its life intimately, its varied social and political aspects, the course of its activity, the character of the men who are prominent in its affairs, and the nature and aims of its influential organizations. We delight our leisure hours with the reading of romance and of the dramatic situations of imaginary life. Not less interesting, not less dramatic, is the actual life of our own communities if only we will understand it. To understand it, if a man be healthy-minded and well-disposed, is to appreciate responsibility. It is most unworthy to take advantage, in self-enrichment, of the opportunities of our democratic life and to refuse to bear our share of its burdens. Against cupidity we must ever set up the standards of honour, and the more sincerely devoted one is to the cause of his party, the more steadfast should be his opposition to every effort to use party place for private gain. True loyalty to party is not loyalty to selfish manipulators. True devotion to the interests of party is not fealty to faction or to the personal ambitions of party managers. True party spirit is opposed to all the baneful practices which emasculate the public service and thus, dishonouring party, lose principles and statesmanship in low intrigue.

My advice would be: Join a party, one of the great parties, according to your general agreement with its record, policy, and tendency; appreciate the necessity and power of political organization and lend your effort to make it wholesome and effective; stand firmly, regardless of your personal fortunes, against every effort to corrupt it or to use it for selfish purpose; support managers who are faithful to the party and serve it for its interests and not their own; stand for honourable candidacies unpurchased and representative of the wisdom and best purpose of the party; in local matters be independent and keep distinct your duty as a member of a national party for the furtherance of national interests, and your duty as a citizen of a local community to aid in having it well governed; stand against "bossism" and all that the word implies, and aim to make your party organization within its proper field representative and its leadership responsible and accountable to the party members.

If you achieve a place of prominence with respect to party management, set yourself against corrupt practices, expose them when you can, and recognize that your highest duty is to the institutions of your country; believe that there is sufficient love of truth and justice to win support for what is well conceived and faithfully declared;

and be content, while making those necessary accommodations of personal opinion, which are essential to co-operative action, to put your faith in the indisputable principles of right conduct which would not be compromised in the open, and in secret purpose and in the undisclosed transsaction should be held equally inviolable. To the extent that these ideals are held sacred, our essential party activities will be a benefit to the Nation.

DEC 5
NOV 5
JAN 8
MAR 4
MAR 18
APR 9
APR 23
MAY 9
FEB 2 2 1973

DARTMOUTH COLLEGE